THE TYRANNY OF TESTING

BANESH HOFFMANN

Foreword by
Jacques Barzun

DOVER PUBLICATIONS, INC.
Mineola, New York

Bibliographical Note

This Dover edition, first published in 2003, is an unabridged republication of the 1964 Collier Books Edition of the work originally published in 1962 by the Crowell-Collier Publishing Company, New York.

Library of Congress Cataloging-in-Publication Data

Hoffmann, Banesh, 1906–
    The tyranny of testing / Banesh Hoffmann ; foreword by Jacques Barzun.
      p. cm.
    Originally published: New York : Crowell-Collier Press, New York, 1962.
    Includes index.
    ISBN 0-486-43091-X (pbk.)
     1. Educational tests and measurements. I. Title.

LB3051.H68 2003
371.26—dc21   2003048898

Manufactured in the United States of America
Dover Publications, Inc., 31 East 2nd Street, Mineola, N.Y. 11501

Acknowledgments

With tests of aptitude and achievement exerting ever greater influence on our lives, people are becoming increasingly uneasy. But their skepticism is held in check by their awe of the professionalism of the testers. The purpose of this book is to dispel that awe by subjecting the testers to public examination. In doing so it can hardly avoid being outspoken. My first thanks go, therefore, to those organizations and their representatives that readily gave me permission to quote sample questions and other material though they knew that my purpose was not flattery: the College Entrance Examination Board, the Educational Testing Service, Harcourt Brace & World, the National Merit Scholarship Corporation, and Science Research Associates.

My thanks go, too, to *The American Scholar, Harper's Magazine,* and *Physics Today,* in which articles of mine appeared from which I here quote.

I am grateful to the many people who have given me permission to quote from their letters and their publications, and to those who read the manuscript in whole or in part and made valuable suggestions. To those colleagues and students whom I have pestered over the years with sample multiple-choice questions and intricate questions about these questions I offer both my apologies and my thanks. And I know no way to express the depth of my gratitude to Jacques Barzun and Konrad Gries for their crucial advice and constant encouragement, not only while I was writing this book but also during the unfolding of the events that led to its being written.

BANESH HOFFMANN

Flushing, New York
June 1962

Foreword

FOR THE PAST thirty months magazines and newspapers have carried a running debate on the theory and practice of testing. By far the greater part of the discussion has consisted of attacks on so-called objective tests, in direct consequence of Mr. Banesh Hoffmann's articles in *Harper's* and *The American Scholar*. Since then academic writers in professional journals have variously said: "I told you so." Doubts and protests long pent up have at last come forth because one man was courageous enough to attack an entrenched position. It is therefore clear that the time is ripe for the full, documented, and reasoned account which Mr. Hoffmann gives in this book of the inadequacies and dangers of mechanical testing.

The vogue of this type of test began after the first world war, during which it had been used by the Army in the hope of rating intelligence and sorting out capacities. Schools and colleges in the 1920's began to give similar tests to their applicants, who, once admitted, were subjected to true-false quizzes instead of the regular essay examinations. Of their own accord, students took whole "batteries" of commercially produced tests to help themselves decide on a career. By the second world war, testing by check-mark was established practice everywhere in American life—in the school system, in business, in the professions, in the administration of law and in the work of hospitals and institutions for the mentally deranged. The production and administration of tests was an industry employing many hard-working and dedicated people.

Half way through this period, in the forties, it was manifestly useless to raise even a question about the value and effect of these tests. When I devoted a short chapter to doing so in *Teacher in America,* describing with precision

7

enough how mechanical tests raised mediocrity above talent, my remarks were ignored or contemptuously dismissed. I was an obscurantist who lacked the scientific spirit. The most charitable view of my madness was that I was the product of a foreign school system well known to be backward and resistant to modern methods.

Now the tide has turned. As the present book shows, it is the testers who are on the defensive, fighting a rearguard action against the irresistible force of the argument which says that their questions are in practice often bad and in theory very dangerous. Given the widespread use of tests built on these shaky foundations, their evils affect every literate person, directly or through his children. More abstractly but no less truly, the fate of the nation is affected by what tests do, first, to the powers of those who are learning, and, second, to the selection the tests make among the potential leaders of thought and discoverers of new knowledge. Read Mr. Hoffmann's remarks on the National Merit Scholarship program.

But while American public opinion is recovering from its infatuation with fallacious "methods" in several realms —not only in the giving of tests but also in the teaching of reading, in the training of teachers, in the defining of school subjects, and in the handling of discipline at home —the formerly backward and resistant countries of Europe are zestfully adopting most of our mistakes. England, Germany, France are frolicking with child-centered schools, the permissive system, and the batteries of tests. A recent report from France shows that a long tradition of sobriety is no protection against an attractive error. In the midst of its grave political preoccupations France has been agitated by the discovery, based on tests, of an untutored "genius," a "future Kepler or Galileo" among the eleven children of a modest family in a village near Lyons. The only skeptics about this discovery are the teenage genius himself, his mother, and his sister. "All that people say about me is nonsense," said Jean Frêne to his interviewer, and he followed up this perceptive remark with a description of what he had done to be ranked with the great minds of the past:

"I took the Army tests and did better than average. That gave me a chance for officer training. I took more tests. The seventeenth test was on reading comprehension. They give you a sentence to read, and on one side four others to match, of which two are nearly alike. You put a cross in the right box. I got 17 out of 20. The colonel who gave me the test asked me if I had been guessing. I said my answers seemed to me the most sensible, so he asked me to try again.

"On another test?"

"No, the same. I made the same answers and this time I got 19 out of 20. I wonder why, because I didn't do anything different. The colonel seemed terribly surprised."—(*L'Express*, March 22, 1962, p. 18)

The colonel is only at the beginning of his own education in these matters. We in the country which originated the game should take care not to be "terribly surprised" at the ease with which self-deception can occur on a national scale. After years of faith in the so-called experiments that proved the validity of the look-and-say method of teaching children how to read, it turns out that the tests (here too) were bad and the results naturally worthless. It is high time to ask what this would-be experimenting in education amounts to. It has long been known in industry that a mere change in the surroundings of production will improve output—temporarily. It is likely that mere change has the same effect in school, and all that the experiments prove is that children respond to novelty in the normal way of increased interest.

With this in mind, the carefully documented recital Mr. Hoffmann gives of the way in which the manufacturers of tests defend their product takes on a new importance. For it shows that in contemporary societies the trappings of science are readily used, in good faith, to produce disastrously false results. These results become the stock-in-trade of vested interests. When doubts are uttered, money and prestige are threatened, and indeed all of society is shaken, at least in its easy assumptions. As Mr. William Whyte showed in *The Organization Man,* testing in personnel work does something very different from what was generally thought; and as Mr. Hoffmann shows in the book before us, testing in school and college does the very opposite of what was hoped. In the one case the method represses individuality; in the other it misreads performance.

Every citizen and parent should remember the links in this characteristic chain, which begins with method and ends with gadgetry, whenever proposals come before boards of education to set up large and expensive systems, whether of tests, television courses broadcast from airplanes, or teaching machines. The acts of learning and teaching are more subtle, delicate, elusive, than any method so far found. The desire to teach great numbers does raise difficulties correspondingly great. But it is no solution to do something next door to what is wanted simply because that something is easier to do. If there was not enough milk for growing children would we distribute tap water? Or give them free vaccination against smallpox? Though this is not precisely the analogue of what we have done in the matter of examining the young learner's knowledge, it is precisely true of the arguments used in support of mechanical testing: it is easier and cheaper than the method of confronting mind with mind through the written word.

The further argument that essay examinations cannot be graded uniformly, even by the same reader, only shows again the character of mind itself: it is not an object to be weighed or sampled by volume like a peck of potatoes or a cord of wood. Variations in performance and estimate will always subsist. Hence an objective test of mind is a contradiction in terms, though a fair test, a searching examination, a just estimate, are not. Among the tests that are unfair, certainly, are those which penalize the finer mind—as Mr. Hoffmann proves—and those which, through the forceful presence of wrong answers, may divert that mind from the accurate knowledge it possessed a moment before. Anyone who has suddenly doubted the spelling of a word which he was about to write correctly will recognize how easily doubt can work distraction upon thought.

Again, the frequent observation that nowadays the ablest students are the least well prepared (the foolishly called "under-achievers") may well have its source in the neglect of effort which mechanical testing entails. A pupil does not really know what he has learned till he has organized and explained it to someone else. The mere recognition of what is right in someone else's wording is only the beginning of the awareness of truth. As for the writing of essays—and the art of correcting them—excellence can of course not be achieved without steady practice, which, once again, the fatal ease of mechanical testing tends to discourage. But if the tendency of such tests is to denature or misrepresent knowledge, to discourage the right habits of the true student, and to discriminate against the original in favor of the routine mind, of what use are such tests to a nation that has from its beginnings set a high value on instruction and the search for truth? There is no ready answer that is not invidious to the makers of tests. But they too are in good faith, which is why it is urgent and important to study their claims as does Mr. Hoffmann, and decide for oneself on which side objectivity does in fact lie.

JACQUES BARZUN

June 30, 1962

Contents

Chapter 1

A Little Learning Is a Dangerous Thing:
☐ True ☐ False

ON THE OTHERWISE unmemorable day, Wednesday, March 18, 1959, the *Times* of London printed the following letter to the editor:

Sir,—Among the "odd one out" type of questions which my son had to answer for a school entrance examination was: "Which is the odd one out among cricket, football, billiards, and hockey?"

I said billiards because it is the only one played indoors. A colleague says football because it is the only one in which the ball is not struck by an implement. A neighbour says cricket because in all the other games the object is to put the ball into a net; and my son, with the confidence of nine summers, plumps for hockey "because it is the only one that is a girl's game." Could any of your readers put me out of my misery by stating what is the correct answer, and further enlighten me by explaining how questions of this sort prove anything, especially when the scholar has merely to underline the odd one out without giving any reason?

Perhaps there is a remarkable subtlety behind it all. Is the question designed to test what a child of nine may or may not know about billiards—proficiency at which may still be regarded as the sign of a misspent youth?

Yours faithfully,
T. C. BATTY

This question of the four sports makes a fascinating party game. There are many reasons for picking the various answers, and one has only to read the question aloud to start a party off in high gear, with everyone joining in the fun. Any number can play. There is only one drawback: after a while the fun suddenly stops and the party becomes indignantly serious. This happens as soon as someone asks what sense there is in giving children such questions on tests; for then, right away, the fat is in the fire. Parents begin recalling similar questions that their own children had on tests. College students complain that such questions are by no means confined to children. Graduate students and older people push the age limit higher as they recount their own experiences. And soon there is an awed realization that there may, in fact, be no age limit at all.

But before the party reaches this solemn stage—and before this book does—there is fun to be had. Even the staid London *Times* could not resist enjoying it. On March 19, the day after the appearance of Mr. Batty's letter, it printed the following two letters, in this order, without comment:

Sir,—"Billiards" is the obvious answer . . . because it is the only one of the games listed which is not a team game.

Because the answer is so simple and does not require the child answering it to have a detailed knowledge of the games referred to, I should have thought it a very suitable question for an intelligence test.

Sir,— . . . football is the odd one out because . . . it is played with an inflated ball as compared with the solid ball used in each of the other three [games].

At this stage I managed to tie myself into an intellectual knot that still has me slightly bewildered. When I had read these three letters it seemed to me that good cases had been made for football and billiards, and that the case for cricket was particularly clever, but that the case for hockey was dubious at best. At first I thought this made hockey easily the worst of the four choices and, in effect, ruled it out. But then I realized that the very fact that hockey was the only one that could be thus ruled out gave it so striking a quality of separateness as to make it an excellent answer after all—perhaps the best.

Fortunately for my peace of mind, it soon occurred to me that hockey is the only one of the four games that is played with a curved implement. But what if I had not thought of that? The problem haunts me still.

In the meantime, the *Times* had not been idle. On March 20th it published the following letter from an eminent philosopher:

Sir,—Mr. T. C. Batty . . . has put his finger on what has long been a matter of great amusement to me. Of the four— cricket, football, billiards, hockey—each is unique in a multitude of respects. For example, billiards is the only one in which the colour of the balls matters, the only one played with more than one ball at once, the only one played on a green cloth and not on a field, the only one whose name has more than eight letters in it. Hockey is the only one ending in a vowel. And so with each of the others.

It seems to me that those who have been responsible for inventing this kind of brain teaser have been ignorant of the elementary philosophical fact that every thing is at once unique and a member of a wider class. Mr. Batty's son, in his school class, could be underlined as the only member who was Mr. Batty's son. Similarly with every member of his class.

The next day the *Times* printed a tongue-in-cheek letter of typically British insularity, based as it was on the purely amateur status of hockey in the British Isles:

Quite clearly "hockey" is the correct answer. . . . Every child should know that of the four games quoted hockey is the only example of one which, at present, no player is ever paid to play. The examiners are plainly anxious to discover how aware the child is of the problems of choosing a career."

Finally, after a day of meditative silence, the *Times* grew more serious and printed this letter:

Sir,—In reply to Mr. Batty's letter . . . I wonder if he would be interested in the results I obtained from a class of 11-year-old children of more than average intelligence and who recently sat for the common entrance examination for secondary education?

I asked them to choose the "odd one out" and then to give their reasons for doing so. The results were as follows:— Football 18, Billiards 17, Hockey 3, Cricket 1.

The reasons they gave were mainly those already submitted by Mr. Batty.

I agree with your correspondent and wonder how far this question and questions of a similar nature are a true and reliable guide in the testing of intelligence.

Having enjoyed its romp and returned full circle to the crucial, fun-dampening question, the *Times* dropped the whole topic from its letter columns. The incident was over, and an opportunity for action had been lost.

But the crucial question is with us still: what sense is there in giving tests in which the candidate just picks answers, and is not allowed to give reasons for his choices? We can not dismiss this as primarily a British problem. The United States is far in advance of all other countries in its reliance on tests of this sort. Here there is no escaping the testers with their electrical scoring machines. They measure our IQ's at regular intervals and assess our scholastic achievement throughout our school days. They stand harsh guard at the gateway to National Merit Scholarships, and they tell admissions officers how many points' worth of college aptitude we possess. They pass on our qualifications for graduate study and entry to professional schools. They classify us en masse in the army. They screen us when we apply for jobs—whether in industry or government. They are even undertaking to certify our worth when we come up for promotion to positions far outranking their own.

The majority of the questions that the testers ask are clear-cut and straightforward. But too often ambiguity creeps in, as it did in the "four-sports" question. While that question may not have been appropriate for an entrance examination in England, it is not entirely without value. There is one place at least where it could serve a useful purpose—fairyland. One wonders why it has not been used there already. In those tales where three brothers vie for the hand of a princess, for instance, could one hope for a safer and more efficient elimination device than this "four-sports" question? Let the first suitor say "football," or "billiards," or "cricket," or "hockey"—it really does not matter which—and the king, without thinking, can justly say, "Off with his head." When the youngest brother, the good one, undaunted by the fate of his elders, comes forward to make his choice, all he has to do—and even with his proverbial lack of guile he would do it instinctively, as would you or I—is to pick an answer that has not been chosen previously. At once the king can embrace him there in public with a happy cry of joy—a cry echoed weakly by the tremulous lips of the princess— and say to him, "Take her. She is yours. And with her, half my kingdom." It makes a lovely scene. No test question need ever be discarded as useless.

But for testing purposes in real life many questions should be discarded. Many questions are indeed discarded in the long and difficult process of constructing a multiple-choice test. Yet questions survive that are worse than useless; they are, indeed, positively harmful.

For example, I am told that on a certain test a question appeared of which the following is the gist:

Emperor is the name of
  (A) a string quartet
  (B) a piano concerto
  (C) a violin sonata

This seems to be a simple, straightforward question. The average student quickly picks answer B and proceeds untroubled to the next question, perhaps feeling elated at being given so simple a test. But what of the superior student? He knows of the *Emperor Concerto* of Beethoven, but he also knows of the *Emperor Quartet* of Haydn; and his knowledge puts him at a disadvantage, for because of it he must pause to weigh the relative merits of answers A and B while his more fortunate, less well-informed competitors rush ahead.

In this particular case the superior student does not ponder long. Two theories occur to him: the examiner is malicious, or the examiner is ignorant of the Haydn work. If this is the first dubious item that he has encountered on the test, he inclines to the second alternative and chooses answer B with little delay.

Yet even in this simple case he suffers a penalty far exceeding the slight loss of time. For he has been led to call into question both the good will and the competence of the examiner; and this subjects him to a psychological handicap, the severity of which will depend on how faulty or impeccable is the rest of the test. No longer is it possible for him to skim innocently ahead. Instead, he must proceed warily and dubiously, ever alert for intentional and unintentional pitfalls. And whenever he comes to a question for which he, with his superior ability, sees more than one reasonable answer, he must stop to evaluate afresh the degrees of malice and incompetence of the examiner. Such a test becomes for the superior student a highly subjective exercise in applied psychology—and, if he is sensitive, an agonizing one.

Let me illustrate how painful and upsetting this mistrust of the good will and competence of the examiner can be. To do this it is necessary to set a trap, for which I beg the reader's forgiveness in advance. Consider the following multiple-choice question, which is not an unfair imitation of test items of its type. The problem is to pick, from among the five choices, that pair of words which best fits the meaning of the sentence as a whole when the first word of the pair is inserted in the first blank in the sentence and the second word of the same pair is inserted in the second blank in the sentence:

The American colonies were separate and .... entities, each having its own government and being entirely
....

(A)	incomplete	—	revolutionary
(B)	independent	—	interrelated
(C)	unified	—	competitive
(D)	growing	—	organized
(E)	distinct	—	independent

Your response to this question will be colored by your attitude toward me. Suppose I had not warned you that I was setting a trap. Then you would doubtless quickly pick answer E on the grounds that "separate" calls for "distinct," and "having its own government" for "independent," while with doubtful choices, such as B, the second word offered throws the obvious meaning of the sentence into complete confusion.

But I did warn you that I was setting a trap. And this makes you wary and less confident. How good does answer E seem when you examine it more critically, bearing in mind the possible existence of intentional and unintentional

pitfalls? The word "distinct" does not contribute significantly to the sentence. After "separate" it seems almost
unnecessary, except as the completion of a cliché.

Perhaps redundancy is being asked for, since the directions do call for the words that best fit the meaning of the
sentence as a whole. This is a comforting theory. But
the trouble with it is that one does not know the meaning
of the sentence as a whole till one knows the whole sentence. So the call for redundancy is by no means clear.

Besides, there is the word "independent." Although it
does, at first glance, seem to go with "having its own
government," thereby contributing a further element of
redundancy, can you ignore the force of the word "entirely" that precedes it? "Entirely" is a strong word. Is it
likely that I included it accidentally? (Actually I included
it intentionally.) Were the colonies "entirely" independent? Were they not rather "interdependent"? Come to
think of it, what about the word "colonies" itself? Does
it pertain to the period after the War of Independence?
If not, then the colonies were not independent of the
crown, and therefore certainly not "entirely independent."
The force of the word "entirely" might have escaped you
had you thought there was no wile in the question. But
now you are deterred by it; and worried, too, by the
tautology that would result if you ignored it and chose
answer E on the assumption that "independent" was
meant to imply only a limited type of political independence corresponding to the fact that each colony had its
own government.

Since answer E begins to look dubious when you subject it to mistrustful scrutiny, you now examine the other
choices again. But the "entirely" spoils them all, and you
declare that there is no correct answer.

Unfortunately, this does not release you from the re-
quirement of making a specific choice. The rules of this
particular type of multiple-choice question call on you to

pick the "best" answer, even though having to do so is a hardship when no answer is even good.

How do you go about picking the "best" answer here? Perhaps you reject answer B on purely grammatical grounds, since "each" does not go well with "interrelated" —although you could not safely do even this had there been a grammatical error in the directions. You then study the other answers carefully, trying to decide which one is least objectionable.

Suppose in the end you realize that answer D is that one. You still cannot help wondering whether answer D was the one you were really supposed to pick, for you find yourself involved in a subjective guessing game, wondering not which answer is intrinsically the "best" but, instead, which answer the poser of the question may happen to think is "best."

Perhaps this is not a simple, straightforward question of the sort that you would be happy to see on a multiple-choice test. But it is certainly not a grossly unfair caricature.

*   *   *

Actually the above question is taken verbatim from a descriptive booklet, *Scholastic Aptitude Test,** published in 1956 by the College Entrance Examination Board. The question is number 17 and it appears on page 24, where it is said to be "easy because the answer words directly parallel the meaning of words already in the sentence." The wanted answer is E, and the reasons given to justify this choice are, except for minor paraphrase, those in favor of E that I presented immediately following the question.

---

* The full title of the booklet is *A Description of the College Board Scholastic Aptitude Test*. For convenience, it is referred to throughout this book by the abbreviated title above. Quotations from this and other booklets published by the College Entrance Examination Board are made with the permission of the Board.

I have tried this question on several of my colleagues. Some pick answer E and are taken aback when I point out, for example, the force of the word "entirely." But what is significant is that, by and large, those who work in relevant fields, such as history, sociology, and English, complain spontaneously that the question is defective, and that when they are pressed for a definite choice they tend to favor D. They see little merit in answer E; and when they are told that this is the wanted answer and that the question is intended to measure scholastic aptitude, they become quite vehement about its shortcomings.

Here is a convenient tool for an interesting experiment. Show this discussion to a colleague, especially one with a feeling for words; let him read as far as the line of asterisks, and then ask him his opinion of the question. Had you shown him this question in the booklet *Scholastic Aptitude Test,* he might have been biased in its favor, believing that any question regarded as easy by an outstanding group like the College Entrance Examination Board must surely be free from serious defect. When you show him the identical question as here presented, you remove this possible bias, perhaps replacing it with an opposite one—yet a legitimate one, for it corresponds roughly to the bias of the student who has found cause to mistrust the good will or competence of his examiner.

Not all people who study this "colonies" question regard it as seriously defective. But this fact does not make it acceptable. If a sizable number of qualified, intelligent people believe a question to be so worded that the wanted answer is unacceptable, that is sufficient reason for branding the question defective, for there will be intelligent examinees who will realize the same thing, and they will be penalized for their perspicacity.

There is more to tell about this particular question, but it must wait till a later chapter. Meanwhile here is a question, sent to me by a correspondent, that nicely illustrates how the superior candidate can be penalized. It is a true-false question that appeared on an IQ test. It seems straightforward and purely factual. According to my correspondent, the question went essentially as follows, and for the sake of argument let us take it to be precisely as stated here:

George Washington was born on February 22, 1732
☐ True   ☐ False

The person who has superficially memorized the date, unhesitatingly picks *True*. But George Washington was born before 1752, the year in which Great Britain, and thus also its colonies (which were, of course, not "entirely" independent), changed over to the modern Gregorian calendar. According to the Julian calendar used at the time of Washington's birth, and thus according to contemporary records of that event, he was born on February 11, not February 22. Which answer, then, should one pick: *True* or *False*? Remember: no explanations are allowed. One must simply pick an answer. Picking both answers would not be a wise move. Doing so would not be regarded as evidence of superior ability. It would probably be counted as cheating.

Chapter 2

The Business of Testing

WHAT SENSE is there in giving tests in which the candidate just picks answers without any opportunity to give reasons for his choices?

Let us not jump to the hasty conclusion that there is no sense in it at all. Modern testers, especially those in the United States, rely heavily on multiple-choice tests, and they do so for reasons that, to them, are scientifically compelling. Nor are they alone in their opinions. Many people to whom they explain these reasons are enormously impressed by their seeming cogency, often more so than the testers themselves. Considering the weaknesses inherent in the multiple-choice format, it is clear that the decision to use multiple-choice tests in the first place, and then to place ever greater reliance on them, must have been powerfully motivated.

Having fun at the expense of tests and testers is not mere idle amusement. It serves an important purpose. And exhibiting and analyzing defective questions serves an even more important purpose, as will be seen later on. The problem of testing is far too serious and far too difficult to be treated wholly in a spirit of fun. Two facts dominate the problem. One is that testing must take place.

29

And the other is that, except in the simplest situations, there is no satisfactory method of testing—nor is there likely to be. Human abilities and potentialities are too complex, too diverse, and too intricately interactive to be measured satisfactorily by present techniques. There is reason to doubt even that they can be meaningfully measured at all in numerical terms. Yet measurement, assessment, estimation, guesswork—call it what you will—can not cease.

Decisions about people have to be made every day. Sometimes only a few candidates are involved. Sometimes the number is overwhelming. When we choose a President of the United States, for example, usually only two of the candidates have a reasonable chance of being elected. Whatever we may think of our method of choosing between them—it is certainly not one that we would call "scientific"—it is at least a method, and it yields a decision that is accepted as binding. Before these two candidates are presented to us for our final choice, they have themselves been picked from a larger number of aspirants. Here the manner of choice is more haphazard. No one pretends it is perfect. But it yields decisions, and the decisions are usually final.

Doubtless, by giving the matter moments of serious thought, we could come up with more rational methods of choice. We might, for instance, take our cue from the Fairy Queen in *Iolanthe* as she decrees terrible punishment for the members of England's House of Lords:

> Peers shall teem in Christendom,
>   And a Duke's exalted station
> Be attainable by Com-
>   petitive Examination!

There are, after all, tests constructed by experts which, so they tell us, measure intelligence, knowledge, aptitude, personality, and the like, and measure them in an objective way. We could subject the candidates to tests of this sort and publish their scores for all to see. We could go even further and eliminate from the contest all aspirants whose scores on the various tests did not fall within maxima and minima set objectively by a national committee of test psychologists. Once we give our imaginations free rein all sorts of alluring prospects come to mind. What more logical final step, for instance, than to leave the whole decision to the test experts?

For some reason we shrink from so "scientific" a solution. We feel safer with our present system, imperfect though it be. The rough-and-tumble survival-of-the-fittest selection process that goes on in political life has a certain validity. Despite the danger that demagogues may bewitch the populace, despite the average voter's lack of expert knowledge, despite the irrationality and irrelevance of some of the arguments with which even the best candidates appeal to the people, we prefer our present system. We prefer it not because we believe that it invariably picks the best possible man, but for what, so far as the immediate task of selection is concerned, are mere side effects: as a conspicuous example, that it keeps the man who is elected responsive, in some measure, to the will of the people. It is precisely because we value the side effects so highly that we tolerate, and even cherish, the present process of selection. *There is more to selection than just selection.*

However, we do not always favor selection by popular vote. Sometimes the side effects are unimportant or undesirable. We do not decide by popular vote who shall be permitted to practice medicine or law, for example. We recognize our limitations and insist that the decisions be made by people who are expert in these fields. Nor do we demand to be permitted to vote for candidates for scholarships or admission to college. We prefer to leave these difficult decisions to scholars and other qualified people.

To appreciate the task these people face, let us ask ourselves how we might go about estimating the worth of a candidate for college admission. A prime source of information, obviously, would be his teachers. They could tell us what they thought of his intelligence, his accomplishments, his interests, his drives, his originality, his honesty, his ability to rebound after defeats, and his charm or lack thereof. We could also study the record of his grades in school and his position in his class. We could consider his extracurricular school activities. We could enquire about his health, both physical and mental. We could have him tell us something about himself by asking him to fill out questionnaires and to write about his aspirations and his reasons for wanting to go to college. We could ask for testimonials from people who know him —mostly friends of the family. We could ask about his parents' accomplishments, their backgrounds, whether they had gone to college, whether they maintained an intellectual atmosphere in the home, whether it was a relatively happy home or a home broken by divorce, or perhaps by death.

Seeking to discover what the candidate is like as a person, we would first ask for his photo—though just what use we planned to make of it when we got it we might find difficult to say. And then we would interview him.

So far, so good. But let us not congratulate ourselves just yet. Is all this accumulated information as valuable as it seems? Testimonials from friends of the family can hardly be regarded as trustworthy. Even testimonials from teachers are hard to evaluate. Different teachers have different standards, and some have a natural tendency to write glowing reports while others are inclined to restraint.

What of the student's recital of his aspirations and his list of reasons for wanting to go to college? Are they not more likely to be testimonials to his parents' skill in sensing what will please admissions officers than exercises in ascetic veracity and candid self-analysis?

The interview? It depends on the interviewer and how much time he has, not to mention his insight and experience. And who is to tell how one interviewer's conclusions compare with another's?

The details of his home life? Surely they are subsidiary information at best. More pertinent would be specific evidence of strength of character, initiative, and creativity.

There remains his school record. His grades, his grade average, the courses he took, his rank in his class—these are valuable indications. Yet even they are suspect. Different schools have different standards. The top student in a weak school or a small school may be no better than the fiftieth in a strong school or a large one. We might try rating the different schools by comparing the college records of their graduates with the grades they made in high school. But even this could be unfair. If statistics show that the best students in school X are generally no better than the average students in the renowned High School of Performing Arts and High School of Science, may we not be reluctant to think a student from the former superior to the best of the latter?

Caught in this quicksand of treacherous data, we seek a uniform standard. And we find it—or so we think—in a written entrance examination. All must take the examination who seek entry to our college. Thus at last shall we be able to measure our candidate accurately against his competitors.

But shall we? Different schools prepare students differently. Some schools may make their students cram for the entrance examination, thus giving them an advantage over students from schools that prefer to remain faithful to nobler educational ideals. This thought gives us pause, not only because it casts doubt on the accuracy of our entrance examination as a measuring instrument, but because it reminds us that entrance examinations have powerful side effects on education.

Again, a student can have an off day when he takes the examination. Or, if he is outrageously lucky, he may be in radiant health on that day and also have studied just the right things the night before. Some students never do themselves justice on written examinations—they just go to pieces. Some students cheat. And what of the students who take stimulants to help them on examinations? Shall we consider their conduct ethical, or condemn it as something akin to the doping of race horses? If we condemn it, shall we then also condemn the use of tranquilizers by students who would otherwise just go to pieces? If so, what of the student who takes an aspirin to ease a headache?

There is more yet: not only do different graders of written examinations have different standards, but the individual grader is not even consistent with himself. And finally, grading written examinations takes time. It has to be done painstakingly by people of experience who know the subject thoroughly. It can not be farmed out to children. Thus when there are hundreds of thousands of candidates, the problem of grading their entrance examinations attains staggering proportions.

What, then, is to be done? Nobody seriously pretends that there is a satisfactory answer. Just think of what is required. Simply placing information about the candidates into folders does no good; we must interpret and assess the mass of shaky evidence. Somehow we must combine the incompatible ingredients, and from the resulting mixture extract, as best we can, the fateful decisions, *yes* or *no*—there being scant place for *maybe*. At first our task is easy. We accept those students we should obviously accept and reject those we should obviously reject. But now the task becomes progressively harder, for in effect we must assign to each of the remaining candidates a single merit number to represent our final judgment of his worth: his rank in the group. To compress all our information about a candidate into a single ranking number is clearly absurd—quite ridiculously irrational. And yet it has to be done. In some cases we can be content with broad approximations. But the closer we come to the borderline between acceptance and rejection the sharper must our pretended accuracy grow, and unfortunately, because many of the best students we accept will also be accepted elsewhere, we can only guess at where this borderline will ultimately be located. Do not envy the admissions officer his job.

Faced with this chaos, we find ourselves lending sympathetic ear to the arguments of the test psychologists. We are inclined to see merit in the idea of the standardized, "objective," multiple-choice test, for it neatly solves the problem of grading, and promises to give us uniform measurements of aptitude and ability. To prevent disagreement over what grade to give, the multiple-choice tester asks the student merely to pick answers. He refuses to let the student explain his choices for a very simple reason: grading the various explanations would cause disagreement among the graders. By making the grading objective he reaps valuable benefits; for example, he can dispense with graders entirely and leave the whole process of grading to machines—a fact certainly not without significance when the number of candidates runs into the hundreds of thousands. His grades, with their aura of arithmetical precision, lend themselves to elaborate numerical studies from which he can extract impressive statistical data, including norms for interpreting scores made on the tests. With his objective techniques he can undertake ambitious projects, such as measuring IQ's on a country-wide, mass-production basis to provide a standardized intellectual rating—a single number—for each student, no matter what his background or tastes. He reaps many other benefits, and we shall discuss them later on. But we have seen enough already to begin to understand why people give tests in which the candidate merely picks answers without any opportunity to give reasons for his choices. We may not feel wildly enthusiastic about such tests. But we are beginning to understand the motives of the professional testers.

"*Professional* testers"? Are there, then, people who make a profession out of testing? There are indeed, just as there are people who make a profession out of teaching. And just as the people who make a profession out of teaching are not all actual teachers but may, for example, be school superintendents or, less directly, textbook publishers, so too are there different types of activities within the testing profession. Indeed, the two professions are sometimes intermingled, as when a person teaches how to test.

Testing used to be a purely amateur activity—amateur, that is, from the point of view of the modern professional tester. In the old days, for example, the business executive would hire men on the basis of little more than references, an interview, and a hunch, and would select people for promotion on the basis of subjective opinions of the men and their work. True, he presumably had expert knowledge of the field in which they would be working, and he may well have been a shrewd judge of men. But to the professional tester, so purely personal a method of selection seems haphazard. Where is the science in it? Where the objective, impersonal measurement of ability and personality by means of well-tried tests? Where the economic use of the executive's valuable time if a professional tester could do the main part, if not all, of the job for him faster and better?

In education, too, as professional testers see it, testing used to be quite unprofessional, being performed by professors and others whose primary skills lay more in research and teaching than in testing. These amateurs would make up their own written examinations and correct them laboriously; they had little uniformity of standards, and next to no interest in obtaining hard facts about the relevance of the grades they gave on these examinations to the abilities of the students they were assessing.

Not all professional testers would put it as harshly as this. The more diplomatic would have kind words for the professors and teachers and business executives, perhaps even professing to see possible merit in their methods in certain special situations while criticizing these methods nonetheless.

Though these amateur methods of the professors and teachers and businessmen are still widely used, they are losing ground to the multiple-choice techniques and special services of the professional testers. Few of the people who take multiple-choice tests give much thought to where the tests come from. Some of these tests are made by individual teachers and professors in emulation of the professional testers, but though the practice is widespread it may still be classed as amateurish since these teachers and professors lack the technical, statistical, and consultative resources on which the best professionals rely so strongly. Not all multiple-choice tests are made up within the schools and other organizations that administer them. Many are bought or rented from outside. Test-making has developed into a large, lucrative, and increasingly competitive business. Tests are now available in enormous variety, in all sorts of subjects, and at several levels of difficulty—and with such competitive overlapping that some test publishers feel it imperative to employ traveling salesmen to promote their wares. In 1960, according to *The New York Times,* it was estimated that psychological testing programs throughout the United States had grown to a point where almost 130,000,000 tests had been given in that year—nearly three tests for every student from first grade to graduate school.

Anyone who has a valid reason for giving a test can probably buy an appropriate one from a test publisher who already has it in stock. Or, for unusual purposes, he can commission a test-making organization to construct a test to suit his special needs, although the cost may run to many thousands of dollars.

One does not just buy *a* test. One buys copies of the test, all neatly and uniformly printed, at so many cents per copy. And with them come instructions on how to use them and much important data of a statistical nature.

One may wonder how secrecy is preserved if tests can be readily purchased. But test-makers are usually careful not to sell copies of their tests to the wrong people—it is, after all, to their own advantage not to compromise the security of their tests. Besides, not all tests are for sale. The more important ones, especially those used in major competitive situations, are for hire only, under strict pledge of secrecy, all copies having to be returned to the test-maker immediately after use; and in some cases the contents of such tests are changed each time they are given.

With the proliferation of tests and test-makers came bewilderment. For where money may be made, charlatans inevitably flock. To some people, making a test seemed a simple way of making a living. The various test-makers were by no means equally competent, nor were their products of equal worth. That much was clear. But which tests were the best? Which no good at all? Not all the eager test-users were competent to tell.

In the early nineteen-thirties there occurred a seemingly unimportant event: Professor Oscar Buros, of Rutgers University, was asked to compile an annual list of newly-published standardized tests. What made this significant was the character of Professor Buros, for he was a man of tenacity and courage. He conducted an exhaustive search that unearthed an unexpectedly large number of tests; and as the nature of his catch revealed itself he became concerned about the chaotic state of the test-making industry. Soon he set himself the task of soliciting copies of tests from the test-makers, sending the tests for candid criticism to both experts on testing and scholars in the subjects of the tests, and publishing the criticisms, not always to the delight of the test-makers, in a *Mental Measurements Yearbook*. Because of financial difficulties, the *Yearbook* did not appear annually. At first Buros had hoped, as he explained in *The Nineteen Forty Mental Measurements Yearbook*, to establish "a test users' research institute with the aid of a substantial grant from one of the large philanthropic foundations interested in serving education. Unfortunately it is easier," he went on, "to interest such foundations in test-construction and test-promotional activities than in a program which would serve test users by making available frankly critical appraisals of standard tests."* He could not get foundation support even for his *Yearbook*. In the face of strong emotional reactions from several of the largest test publishers, he nevertheless persisted, managing to bring out new yearbooks at irregular intervals and gradually gaining for his project the respect, if not the love, of the testing profession. The first *Yearbook* appeared in 1938, the most recent, *The Fifth Mental Measurements Yearbook,* in 1959. The latter yields interesting statistics about the modern testing business: with all variant forms of a test lumped together and counted as a single test, it contains reviews of 957 different tests that had appeared since the publication of the previous *Yearbook* in 1953, most of them of the multiple-choice type; and these tests were produced by some 173 different organizations, of which

---

* The Mental Measurements Yearbooks are published by Gryphon Press, Highland Park, N. J., and the quotations from them that appear here and in later chapters are made with the permission of Oscar K. Buros, editor and publisher of the Yearbooks.

Chapter 3

The Flight from Subjectivity

RIGHTLY OR WRONGLY, we set great store in the ability to express oneself in writing. One way to find out how well a person can write is to ask him to write something. That sounds so obvious as to amount almost to a truism. But there are pitfalls. And it was largely because of these pitfalls that the test psychologists developed their multiple-choice techniques. Let us look at the problem through their eyes.

It would be naive to ask examinees to go home and return a week later with essays on topics of their own choice. The temptation to cheat would be too great. We must ask the candidates to write under examination conditions. So we assemble them at a particular time and allow them a specified number of hours to write their essays. But it would be almost equally naive to let them write on any topic they wished, for they could then come fully prepared, even to the extent of having paid someone to write an essay for the occasion that they could reproduce from memory.

Evidently, we must tell the candidates what topic to write about. But that would clearly be unfair, since different students know different things and have different

43

tastes. So we think of several possible topics and allow the students to choose from among them. But thinking of suitable topics is not easy. Obsessed by the need to be unpredictable, we might find ourselves offering something like this:

Indolence
Beauty as a Criterion
Constitutional Prerogative
How Probable Is the Possible?
Mud

This is a far from exciting list. One might even call it dreary. But there are some natural-born writers—essayists, we would perhaps call them—who can write fluently, persuasively, and brilliantly on any topic whatsoever. However, there are people lacking this tongue-in-cheek fluency who yet can write superbly on topics that interest them. Such people are discriminated against if the list of topics contains nothing that stimulates their creativity.

Again, there is the problem of relevance. The fluent name-any-topic-and-I'll-write-on-it writer sometimes attains his dazzling results by not really writing on the subject. Given the topic "Science in the Middle Ages"— of which he knows nothing—he may write urbanely and wittily about the way in which the average person in the Middle Ages managed to live and die without bothering about science at all.

Relevance is always a problem. There is the classic instance of the student who began his essay on "Indolence" with the words "My parrot's name is Indolence." This is an opening of considerable versatility, requiring only minor adjustment to become applicable to almost any one-word topic. In a desperate situation, it might even be made to fit "Constitutional Prerogative." It has the advantage of allowing the candidate to prepare the rest of his essay beforehand. Its only disadvantage is that, no matter how good that essay might be, it would probably not receive a passing grade.

But where do we draw the line between relevance and irrelevance? If all we are seeking to determine is how well the candidates can write, we can tolerate a high degree of irrelevance so long as it does not smack of sharp practice. But when we give essay examinations in order to determine what the candidates know, as well as how well they can marshal their facts and with what felicity present them, our tolerance of irrelevance must be restrained and we must guard particularly against the danger of being bedazzled by mere superficial fluency.

Even an ugly topic like "Mud" could stimulate a creative person of vivid imagination to write an engrossing dissertation—just as the prosaic topic "Roast Pig" once did. But it would not stimulate all creative people to rise to such heights, and in many people, under examination conditions, it might cause a mental block. In general, the chances are that students writing about "Mud" or "Constitutional Prerogative" (whatever that may be) would produce less ingratiating essays than those writing on, say, "April Showers" or "Piracy in Fact and Fiction." And this is the first of the difficulties with essay examinations: some topics tend to attract better grades than others.

A related difficulty is that mere handwriting affects grades. What grader, faced with anywhere from a dozen to a couple of hundred essays, will be able to resist feeling grateful for clear handwriting and allowing his gratitude to influence his judgment? And what grader, struggling to decipher a crabbed, illegible blot-besplattered script, will not, because of it, value the less what he is reading? Graders are not machines, you know. They have their human feelings.

Even poor punctuation or errors of spelling can lessen the esteem a grader feels for what he is reading, though these are actually secondary matters little related to the content and style of the essay. And this brings us to a central difficulty that bedevils judgment. The test psychologists have a technical name for it; they call it the *halo effect*. Our low opinion of a candidate's spelling tends to lower our opinion of his writing ability. If we have known a student in class, our high or low opinion of his abilities tends to raise or lower our rating of his essay. Even his personal neatness or his unpleasant personality can influence the grade we give his essay. A rating of a single skill is not a self-contained thing. It carries a halo that colors other ratings.

The halo effect is akin to prejudice, which too can play havoc with our judgment of an essay.

That different graders have different standards has already been mentioned. The test psychologists have studied this phenomenon carefully. They take, for example, a single essay and ask various qualified people to grade it. The discrepancies in the grades are frightening. The test psychologists tell us that a single essay can receive all grades from A to F when graded independently by different graders. We all know one person may be an easy marker and another a tough one. But how shall we assess a B from one against a D from the other?

There is an even more disturbing fact than this lack of uniformity in the standards of different graders—more disturbing because it is less expected. An individual grader will be inconsistent even with himself—and not just *an* individual grader, but virtually every individual grader. One's own standards change. They are not firmly anchored. There are two different effects involved here. The first is immediately apparent to anyone who grades examinations. His standards change as he reads them. Partly, this is because the sheer drudgery of reading essay after essay after essay blunts the sensibilities. What may, at the start, have seemed to be a fresh and novel approach, when met again in other essays will seem to be more banal. A steady diet of even the most dazzling wit can pall. We all know how disappointing a book of witticisms can be if we read it in a single sitting instead of savoring it intermittently.

Sometimes the essays will tend to set their own standards. The first few may seem atrocious and be graded accordingly. But if succeeding ones are no better, it is a rare grader who can maintain the rigor of his original standards. It is always a salutary experience for the grader, at the end of his task, to reread the early papers without looking at the grades he assigned them and see what he now thinks the essays are worth.

The second effect here is one of time. Let a grader, after several months, read again the essays he once graded, not looking at his former grades but assessing the essays anew. He will find surprising disparities. We might expect, perhaps, that all the grades would tend to be a little higher or lower than before, for though a grader might not be expected to retain an absolute standard, we feel he ought to be able to retain at least a relative one. But some of the essays formerly rated good will now be rated mediocre while essays formerly regarded as merely acceptable will now be rated excellent. This too the test psychologists have demonstrated.

There is even worse to be told. When grades on outside essay examinations are compared with teachers' opinions of their students' abilities, the agreement is apt to be none too good. Naturally, we would not expect that one teacher's standards would match another's. But we are not talking here just of the ratings made by different teachers. We are talking also of rankings made by individual teachers of the students in their individual classes.

Such, then, in outline is the test psychologists' indictment against essay examinations; and it is supported by detailed statistical studies. It is directed not just against essay examinations used for determining who can write well and who not, but, essentially, against all essay examinations. And much of it applies, though perhaps with less force, to examinations that are not quite full-fledged essay examinations but call for short answers to questions ranging from "The Father of his Country was . . ."— a badly worded question, incidentally—to "State briefly the aims of the New Deal and the methods by which Roosevelt sought to achieve them."

If you are still not convinced of the difficulty of grading essay questions, pause here a moment to consider how you would grade this seemingly simple "Father of his Country" question. Presumably the answers "Washington" and "George Washington" would receive equal credit, even though the second is more detailed than the first. But how would you rate unexpected answers like "Gandhi," "Atatürk," "Moses," and "Lenin"? Or safe answers like "a great military leader," "a great leader," or "a good man"? And what of "born on February 22," and "born on February 11," either of which shows that the student had Washington in mind, and suggests that the student had the ability to sense the awkwardness and banality of the sentence "The Father of his Country was Washington"? Should not his taste and originality be specially rewarded? The above are but a few of the possible answers to this ill-conceived question. It is easy to think of others equally apt—and even harder to grade.

What to do? Well, some of the difficulties can be partly overcome. For example, the essay topics can certainly be made better than those given above. Attempts can be made to improve uniformity of grading standards by training people to grade according to certain formulas and by supplying them with sample essays from very poor to very good to illustrate what each grade is meant to signify. Each essay can be graded by more than one person, and the grades averaged. Yet even at best distrust of essay grades remains. There is always gnawing doubt that some of the grades may be unfair; that the same essay might receive a different grade under different circumstances. Indeed, it is more than a doubt. It is a certainty.

There is an incident in the life of the late Mazo de la Roche, author of the best-selling series of novels about the Whiteoak family, that is not without relevance here. She submitted *Jalna,* the first of the series, as an entry in *Atlantic Monthly's* $10,000 novel contest in 1927. It was one of 1,150 manuscripts that the judges had to "grade." A reader for the magazine placed it in the rejection pile. Then, according to *The New York Times,* its handsome binding attracted one of the editors, who picked it up, glanced at the story and did not put it down until he had finished it. The novel won the prize.

If the principal difficulty with essay examinations is the variability of judgment, let us eliminate this subjective element from the process of grading, and produce "objective" tests. So argued the test psychologists. And one of their early ideas was to construct tests with true-false questions like this:

Milk is white: ☐ True ☐ False

With each test they provided a key, telling, for each question, whether the answer *true* or the answer *false* should be counted as correct. The grading could now be done uniformly, the only danger being that a grader might make an error in checking or tallying. But grading could now be done so quickly that there was no great hardship involved in doing it a second time to catch such errors.

The test psychologists could claim many advantages for the true-false format. For example, the new technique of testing, by not requiring the student to write any words, did more than just remove the influence of handwriting on the grade. It saved the student valuable time, thus making for more efficient use of the testing period. More material could be covered. And instead of such estimates as A, B, C, D, and F, the tests yielded sharp numerical grades.

After a while the testers began to realize that true-false questions are of limited scope, being almost always triflingly factual and quite often ambiguous—something that had been evident to scholars all the while.

However, it was perhaps no mean achievement on the part of the test psychologists to have produced a device that so readily combines the factual with the ambiguous and imprecise, especially when it yields grades of such numerical nicety.

It is not difficult to see what is wrong with true-false tests. The easiest way is to try to make up some true-false questions for ourselves. Suppose we try

The sky is blue: ☐ True   ☐ False

That is obviously no good. The sky is sometimes blue, but not always. This gives us an idea, though. We change the question to read

The sky is always blue: ☐ True   ☐ False

This one seems all right. We can not imagine a person seriously denying that the correct answer is *false*. Even if he wanted to quibble that "the sky" might refer to the blue sky in a particular painting we could quibble back that "always" can mean "forever" and that the painting will not last that long. But suppose he argued that to an aviator just above the clouds the sky is indeed always blue. Would we have the ready wit to point out immediately that it is not blue at night? And would we feel absolutely sure of ourselves even if we did? For example, when it is night in one place it is day in another, and the sky is the sky after all, and the question does not say "all of the sky at the same time." If we thought of this we might begin to lose faith in the question. But then the powerful word "always" would revive our confidence. Will the earth last forever? Has it existed since the beginning of time? Assuredly then the sky is not *always* blue.

Our opponent could still pick holes in our arguments. What about the word "is," for example? But we would brush him impatiently aside, saying we were satisfied that the word "always" made the question a good one, and that if we aimed at perfection we would never—— well anyway, let's not quibble, it's only a test question, not a philosophical wrangle, and we have dozens and dozens more to make up.

Even so, the question is not a good one for a test. For we have used the telltale, giveaway word "always." Students soon learn that, on true-false tests, assertions containing strong, forthright words like "always" or "never" are usually intended as *false,* while those containing hesitant, perhapsy words like "sometimes," "can," or "may" are generally to be regarded as *true.* There are exceptions, of course, but, outside of mathematics and similar subjects, they are usually easily recognized, unless telltale words have been used deliberately to deceive. The general practice now is to avoid such words as far as possible.

From our experience with the "blue sky" question we can appreciate how great the temptation is to rely on telltale words. We shall appreciate it even more by trying to do without them. What sorts of questions can we think of that do not use them?

There are simple factual questions like

Chicago is north of Baltimore: ☐ True ☐ False

though even here we have allowed a trace of ambiguity to enter and would do well to reword it as, say,

Chicago is farther north than Baltimore: ☐ True ☐ False

And there are some mathematical, scientific, and logical questions; for example,

If all A are B and some B are C, then some C are necessarily A:
☐ True   ☐ False

As we read this one over, we may be dismayed to find that we have used two telltale words in it: "all" and "some," the latter twice. But these are not telltale words here. They give no automatic clues to the answer. Indeed, if a student looked to them for such clues he would be puzzled to find them pulling in opposite directions.

But we are putting things off. Can we, outside of these special fields, think of worthwhile true-false questions that are not purely factual, that have depth, and that yet escape ambiguity? Even the superficial "milk is white" question was ambiguous—and seriously so. What chance have we, then, of escaping ambiguity when we seek to incorporate depth, or even just an element of judgment?

Suppose we thought of a question like this:

A principal cause of World War II was England's guarantee to Poland: ☐ True   ☐ False

Would we be satisfied with it? Can we not argue plausibly in favor of both *true* and *false*? In fitting depth and judgment into the true-false format, we do them Procrustean violence.

Few professional testers nowadays have a good word to say for true-false tests, except for extremely limited uses. Nevertheless they are still being used—and sometimes grossly misused. For example, in a reputable college the mid-term examination in a Sociology course consisted of some eighty true-false questions and nothing else, and the final examination solely of a hundred or so. This is far from being an isolated instance of the misuse of true-false tests. Indeed, so narrow is the range of the legitimate use of true-false tests that almost every time they are used they are misused. A sociology professor who gives only true-false tests mocks the intellectual content of his course, and no amount of pleading that he has too many students can cover his betrayal of his academic ideals and obligations. If classes are too large, the remedy is to reduce their size, not to give true-false tests. When the professor bows to expediency and uses these tests he does worse than give the tests an aura of respectability: he undermines a major argument for the reduction of class size.

Not everything is either true or false. Not everything is either black or white. Not every question can be answered either yes or no. It is not for nothing that our language has its ifs and buts, its yets and howevers, its neverthelesses and notwithstandings, its possiblies and probablies and perhapses, and its on-the-other-hands. To free themselves from the strait jacket of the trifling, and too often artificial, true-false dichotomy, the testers went over to multiple-choice tests.

We might describe a multiple-choice test as printed sheets of paper and let it go at that. But that would be absurd. There is far more to a standardized multiple-choice test than just the printed paper. How very much more is apt to be surprising to people who know tests only through having taken them. To appreciate what lies behind the printed sheets, let us observe the elaborate procedure by which the best test-makers construct and evaluate a multiple-choice test.

Such a test usually emerges from an intricate collaboration. The person in charge is apt to be an expert on test-making, usually one trained in psychology. He calls in consultants who are expert in the subject to be tested, and other experts as they are needed. If the test is to be used for screening applicants for a particular job, the first thing to decide is which qualities, aptitudes, and abilities are basic for success in performing the job, and which are undesirable; and with new jobs, like that of astronaut, for which there is little hard experience to go on, these decisions have to be made by shrewd guesswork. Usually, though, enough is already known about the general requirements for success; or, if not, they can be determined by observing, questioning, and testing people who have already been successful in the job.

Let us suppose these matters to have been decided. The next step is to break the various aptitudes and skills into small constituent parts that lend themselves to multiple-choice testing.

When the scope of the test has been determined and its detailed structure mapped out, the test-expert and his committee call upon subject experts to make up appropriate multiple-choice questions. Making up these questions is not at all as easy as it sounds. To be sure, making up multiple-choice questions of sorts is simple enough, but not making good ones. The test expert and his committee are by no means easy to please. They have had considerable experience and can see all sorts of pitfalls that are hidden from ordinary view. They submit all the questions to searching scrutiny. Some they reject outright. Some they make acceptable by careful rewording. Some they reject reluctantly after long struggles to put them into satisfactory shape. There is much discussion between the question-makers and the critical committee. There is haggling over phrases and even over individual words. Feelings may be hurt and tempers may rise. But ultimately a collection of multiple-choice questions comes into being that is reasonably satisfactory to all concerned.

One would think, perhaps, that the main work was now done, and that it was time to start the printing presses. But the process is only begun. No reputable test-maker would market a multiple-choice test at this stage. How could he tell whether the questions were as good as he thought they were? How could he tell whether the test as a whole would perform as it was intended to perform? How could he convince purchasers that the test had merit? There is a great deal more work to be done before the test will be ready for use, much of it routine statistical work that large organizations can often handle more expeditiously than individual entrepreneurs.

The first step is to *pre-test* the questions: to try them out on people comparable to those for whom the tests are intended and to compile a separate statistical dossier for each question.

These dossiers are crucial. They speak directly to the test expert in his own language of statistics. He is at home with them and no longer working in the dark. They give him something objective to go on. If a question is answered correctly mainly by the "better" examinees it is a good question. If it is answered correctly mainly by the "poorer" ones it is a bad question. If a fair number of the "better" examinees favor one answer and a comparable number another answer, the question is probably ambiguous. If nobody gets it right it may be too hard, or the wanted answer may be a wrong answer, but either way it is a bad question. If everyone gets it right, it is useless. And so on.

The pre-test sends noses back to grindstones. More questions are rejected, others are again rewritten, and new ones are constructed that are themselves subjected to pre-testing. The number of questions on each topic is brought into conformity with the estimated relative importance of the topic; and the numerical balance between questions of various grades of objectively determined difficulty is adjusted to the percentage of candidates that the test is designed to reject, or to some other such desideratum. And ultimately a rigorously screened, well-proportioned version of the test emerges.

Is it now ready for use? Not yet. It is given a preliminary tryout, perhaps involving as many as several thousand candidates. Again statistics are gathered, though now they are less concerned with individual questions than with the test as a whole. Scores made on the test are correlated with the abilities of the candidates as determined by other means; or the test may be tried out on older people who already have jobs of the sort that the test is concerned with, and their scores on the test correlated with their degrees of success or failure in the job as estimated, say, by their superiors. Whatever the method used, statistics are gathered and the test is provisionally *validated:* that is to say, its ability to do what it is supposed to do is given a numerical statistical rating.

The *validity* of the test is not its only attribute to receive a numerical rating. Test-experts and test-users alike wish to know also the extent to which they can rely on the test scores. If a person scored 80 out of 100, for example, how likely would it be that his score really should have been 80? Would he score close to 80 on taking the test again, assuming that, by some magic, his score was not affected by his having taken the test before? Suppose another candidate of identical ability and knowledge were to take the test. Would his score also be 80 or might it be markedly higher or markedly lower? If people of comparable ability get widely divergent scores the test has low *reliability;* if they get nearly equal scores the reliability is high.

Because of the dearth of identical twins, it is not easy to determine the reliability of a test directly. Indeed, since identical twins are not completely identical, not even they would yield completely reliable measures of reliability. But there is great desire to know the reliability of a test, and there are various methods of estimating it. For example, the test expert may give the test twice to the same people and compare their scores to see how well the test agrees with its own ratings. Though this method has obvious defects,* it can yield an acceptable estimate of reliability.

Alternatively, the test-expert may give the test just once to each person, and compare the scores made on a selected half of the questions with those made on the other half, applying certain mathematical corrections into which we need not enter. Or he may use yet other methods of a more subtle sort. But, whatever the method or methods, he will come up with a numerical measure of the test's reliability.

The test-expert and his statistical helpers are still not done. One of the beauties of multiple-choice tests, with their sharp numerical grades, is the readiness with which they lend themselves to statistical analysis. Averages are computed, and also standard deviations, and means, and percentiles. Various norms are established. Graphs are drawn. Tables are prepared for converting scores into percentiles and other such purposes. Cutoff scores may be determined for various categories, a person scoring below the appropriate cutoff score being declared an extremely poor risk, percentages perhaps being given to indicate how small is the likelihood of his proving satisfactory.

The test-maker gathers all his statistical data together and presents them, in detailed outline, in a descriptive *manual* along with much other descriptive and technical matter about the test: for example, its aims, the formulas used in computing the statistics, instructions to the prospective user on how to administer the test—including such basic information as the amount of time to allow the candidates and even the exact words to use in explain-

---

* A professor at a leading state university cites the cases of two students each of whom took the multiple-choice *Graduate Record Examination* in physics in November, 1961 and again the following January. In this brief interval one of them raised his rating from the twenty-ninth percentile to the sixty-ninth, the other from the sixty-first to the ninety-fourth. The professor wryly remarks that "from these examples one can draw the conclusion either that the students greatly benefit by repeating the examinations or that the scores are quite meaningless or both."

ing the rules to them before they start—instructions on how to score the test and interpret the results, explanations of the meaning of statistics in general and of the meaning of the statistics about this particular test—all this not perhaps without propagandistic overtones and possibly an innuendo or two about the merits of competing tests.

At last the presses can roll. The test is now ready for sale or for hire. It is sold complete with manual and scoring key, in batches of the desired number of copies of the printed test and answer sheets. If it is too secret a test to be sold outright, it may be rented and the scoring key withheld.

Even now the process of test construction is not necessarily at an end. The test-maker will probably observe the test in actual use and accumulate further statistics; the subsequent performance of successful candidates will be compared with their test scores and the validity of the test recomputed; the manual may be revised; and, if need be, the test itself altered.

Nor is even this necessarily the end of the matter. If the test is of sufficient importance, and intended for widespread use over the years, independent test psychologists may conduct their own statistical investigations of its merits and publish their findings—not always flattering—in technical psychological journals. And, of course, reviews of the test will appear in an issue of the *Mental Measurements Yearbook*.

It is clear from all this that a person buying or renting a multiple-choice test from a reputable test publisher does not get mere printed sheets of haphazardly chosen questions hastily thrown together. He gets a burnished testing instrument of the most modern sort, painstakingly constructed and calibrated on scientific lines by a highly professional team of experts.

Chapter 4

Objectivity and Ambiguity

A BURNISHED testing instrument of the most modern sort, painstakingly constructed and calibrated on scientific lines by a highly professional team of experts. What more could one want?

The professional testers can make a hypnotically plausible case. They have but to compare their rational, scientific procedures with the old, amateur, slapdash methods: business executives asking their colleagues' opinions and then playing a hunch, or harassed teachers thinking up their own essay questions—questions actually calling for written answers, mark you—grading them subjectively as best they could, rarely seeking to discover how well their standards of grading matched those of their fellow teachers, never seeking to determine whether their home-made examinations really picked the best students, never making any scientific studies at all of the merits of their procedures—just relying blindly on fallible, individual judgment.

Put like this the case seems irresistible. How can such amateur guesswork stand up against skilled professionalism, against statistical facts—against Science itself? Indeed, the testers do not hesitate to point out that they have statistics to prove that their tests are clearly more valid and reliable than the older sort.

The test psychologists may not present their case in quite such black-and-white terms. They may, for example, concede merit to essay examinations and pay their respects to the judgment of certain individuals, whether teachers, business executives, or politicians. And they may well go so far as to say that their own tests are far from perfect— using, however, language or tone of voice that suggests extraordinary magnanimity on their part while strengthening the implication that their testing methods are unassailably the best we have.

Among themselves, test psychologists are apt to be quite candid, even to the extent of being bitterly critical of other test psychologists. And the best test-makers sometimes lean over backwards to prevent misinterpretation and misuse of test scores, a distinguished case in point being the detailed books *College Board Scores*, written jointly by the College Entrance Examination Board and the Educational Testing Service. These books, however, barely stray outside the family circle, being addressed primarily to college admissions officers and others who must professionally interpret scores made on College Board tests.

In their public stance the testers generally behave less candidly. And even within the family circle they seem to believe that their scientific routines place them in an impregnable position so far as outside criticism is concerned.

Their case is far from impregnable, though, as is perhaps already clear, for we have allowed irony to enter our presentation of its outline in order to heighten the visibility of some of the weaknesses in the professional testers' position.

It is difficult to know where best to begin a discussion of these weaknesses. Suppose we start with the matter of a name. The testers call their multiple-choice tests "objective tests" and would have us regard objectivity as a virtue. But the term "objective test" is a misnomer. The objectivity resides not in the test as a whole but merely in the fact that no subjective element enters the *process* of grading once the key is decided upon. No matter how abstruse the subject, a child can grade a multiple-choice test. The child need not be gifted, or even have average intelligence. The process of grading is humdrum and calls for no unusual talents.

The professional testers do not like to put it this way. You will not find any of them boasting that their tests can be graded expertly by children; that does not give quite the impression they seek to convey by the phrase "objective tests." They would be horrified if we suggested the alternative term "child-gradable tests," and this not because of any sensitivity on their part to such awkward use of words. Though the testers regard grading by machine as preferable to grading by children—it does sound not only more precise and modern but somehow more dignified and learned—they prefer to play down even this aspect of "objectivity." They would take exception to the term "machine-graded tests," though they would probably do so ostensibly on the ground that their tests do not *have* to be graded by machine since they can be graded by hand—adult hand, they would hasten to add. For, when seeking to sell tests to business concerns, the test-makers do sometimes point out that their tests can be quickly graded by clerks in the office.

To proceed with this matter of objectivity, let us consider the following hypothetical objective question:

The letters A, C, E, G, I are in alphabetical order:
□ True   □ False

Is this an easy question or a hard one? "Easy," you say? But that is only your judgment. The way to tell is to try the question on many people and see how they answer it. Do you still maintain it is easy? That you cannot imagine anyone with any sense at all picking the wrong answer? Doesn't that depend on which is the wrong answer? Suppose the wanted answer were *false*. Then the question would be outstandingly difficult—so difficult that probably no one would get it right. Yet it would be graded objectively.

Now, of course, all this seems like pure fantasy. Let us therefore come down to fact—to legal fact, in fact. I am indebted to Judge Philip Huntington, formerly Justice of the New York State Supreme Court, for bringing to my attention and allowing me to quote a decision he rendered in 1954 in a case involving an examination, prepared by the State Civil Service Commission, for promotion in the police force from patrolman to sergeant. His decision was upheld unanimously by the Court of Appeals.

A group of candidates brought suit, complaining that three questions on the multiple-choice test were defective. In his decision, Judge Huntington wrote in part (I omit his citations of precedents):

Of the three questions involved herein, numbers 51, 55, and 61, I deem the first-mentioned to be beyond the scope of judicial review [the reason for this being given later]; but the "key" answers to the two latter appear to me so contrary to reason and common sense as to cross the border-line into being arbitrary and capricious, in which case, the Court may justly intervene.

Concededly the Court may not interfere in these Civil Service test matters, because it entertains a different opinion of what the best answer is; but the Court may intervene where the "key" answer is arbitrary, capricious, or just plain wrong.

Applying this test to Question 51, which reads as follows:

"51. Evidence of facts from which the commission of a crime may be inferred is called:

    A. circumstantial evidence

    B. direct evidence

    C. presumptive evidence

    D. preferential evidence"

answer "A," the key answer, is not wrong, and neither is "C" the selection contended for by the applicants. The most that can be said, is that it is an unfortunate inclusion of two alternatives, either of which might be chosen by an examinee who knows the subject, but who is unsuccessful in reading the examiner's mind. However, when the key answer is not actually wrong, the administrator's decision of what constitutes the "most acceptable" answer, under the law, must be accepted as final; and it is under this rule that Question No. 51 is not reviewable in this proceeding.

Question 55, which reads as follows:

"Police Departments themselves have gone into the recreation field in the interest of crime prevention principally because

    A. the usual municipal recreational activities are planned for children who conform

    B. it enables them to apprehend delinquents who might otherwise not be caught

    C. they possess the equipment and trained leaders to do the job

    D. it provides a balance and understanding for the police officer to have such an association."

falls in a different category. In none of the authoritative literature which has been furnished to the Court is the "key" answer (A), suggested as the correct answer; and while the answer contended for (D) does not tell the whole story, since it puts the emphasis on the police officer's understanding, instead of the mutual understanding of both policeman and youngster, it at least approximates the truth.

Question 61 reads as follows:

"61. Police Administrators sometimes fail to react favorably to ideas and suggestions presented by employees. Of the following reasons for lack of administrative action or for unfavorable action on a suggestion, the most justifiable would be that

   A. the police administrator has not acted on the rec-
      ommendation of a disinterested staff member as-
      signed to review the suggestion
   B. the suggestion has been improperly prepared or
      presented
   C. the police administrator is too busy with regular
      business matters to give time to the consideration
      of the suggestions made by the staff members
   D. previous suggestions made by the same employee
      have not been worthwhile."

This question has for its key answer (B). Since the preliminary
statement does not postulate, that the idea or suggestion was a
good one, the most natural and justifiable reason for rejecting
it would seem to be that it was no good. If we assume that the
suggestion did have merit, the suggested answer seems pre-
posterous. I am not sure what answer (A) means. It has an
awkward sentence structure so that we cannot tell whether it
means he has not acted *because no action was recommended
by a staff member,* or, that he has not acted, *although action
was recommended by a staff member.* If it means the former,
and probably that is the intended meaning, then that would be
an entirely justifiable reason for inaction, whether the idea had
merit or not.

   Thus, for the reasons enumerated, the application is granted
as to questions 55 and 61 and is denied as to question 51.

   The test was an "objective" one. It had been graded
objectively. Because of complaints made before the trial,
the State Civil Service Commission had agreed to change
its mind about two questions. The test was therefore
graded a second time—again objectively, though this time
with a different outcome. Nor was this a trivially different
outcome. As a result of the new objective grading, nine
candidates who had formerly objectively failed were now
objectively rated as having passed. This, however, did not
satisfy nine other candidates who still were objectively
rated as having failed, and they were the candidates who
brought suit. One presumes that after the law intervened

the test was once more graded objectively, with yet different results.

There is something in this affair that strikes one as curious. Why did the testers appeal the decision? Why did they even let the matter come to court in the first place? Did they really believe that their questions were good? And did they still believe so after reading the judge's opinion? Does their conduct inspire confidence in their suitability as testers of men?

There is another aspect of the professional testers' objectivity that needs to be understood, an aspect that the professional testers prefer not to stress. Consider purely for the sake of illustration, this hypothetical true-false question:

If X is like Y and Y is like Z then X must be like Z:
     □ True   □ False

The superficial student does not need to think about such a question. For him it is obvious, and he immediately picks *true*. But a better student will not be so hasty. He may argue, for example, that X might be a green triangle, Y a green beverage, and Z a red beverage. Since a green triangle is not like a red beverage, he will choose *false*. And we may well feel inclined to agree with him.

What of a really deep student, though? He may go beyond this stage in the argument, realizing the vagueness and elasticity of the word "like." Though a green triangle does not superficially resemble a red beverage, each has something in common with a green beverage, and in this sense the two have an element of likeness. The same is true of any X, Y, and Z. If X is like Y, and Z is also like Y, then X and Z have in common, if nothing else, that each is like Y. So the deep student, working at this level of sophistication, picks *true*.

It does not matter whether the wanted answer is *true* or *false*. In either case, the question will be graded objectively. And in either case the superficial student and the deep student will receive identical scores.

Any competent person who has ever graded a non-objective mathematics or science examination knows that a correct answer obtained by incorrect methods is worth very little, while a wrong answer obtained by correct methods can deserve a top score; and even that a wrong answer obtained by wrong methods can be indicative of outstanding ability, and merit a bonus score. For example, the problem as stated in the examination might be a fairly straightforward one, but the student might misread it as a much harder problem. This harder problem might actually be beyond the capabilities of even the best students at his level to solve. But if he nevertheless made a brilliant attempt, and if this attempt failed because of subtle reasons that he could not be expected to perceive, then the wise examiner who knew his subject well would realize that he was dealing with a student of unusual ability.

Similarly, any competent person grading a non-objective examination in history, sociology, and the like, will know that an incorrect conclusion arrived at by excellent arguments must be regarded as having far greater merit than a correct conclusion arrived at by appalling illogic, and will assign his grades accordingly.

But the professional objective testers ignore all this. They are concerned only with the final choice, not with the quality of the reasoning that led to it. They are prepared to make enormous sacrifices for the sake of achieving objectivity. If essay testers and interviewers and players of hunches were prepared to make equivalent sacrifices they too could achieve comparable objectivity, numerical nicety, and pseudo-scientific decorum.

It is for reasons such as those discussed in this chapter that scholars refer to these tests not as objective tests but as "objective" tests.

All but the most unimaginative have sensed ambiguity in multiple-choice tests they have taken. But the average examinee hesitates to believe that his judgment may be better than that of the test-maker and that the ambiguity he senses really exists. After all, the test he is taking is handsomely printed. It has an air of professionalism. And the organization administering it presumably has faith in it. How, then, could it contain ambiguities? Surely the test-maker would have eliminated all genuine ambiguities. The seeming ambiguities must arise from the candidate's imperfect understanding of the subject. If he knew more about it the ambiguities would vanish.

But if the candidate thinks in this way, he is mistaken. The ambiguities do exist. And the more one knows about the subject the more glaring they tend to become.

By no means are all multiple-choice questions ambiguous. But the very format invites ambiguity, and invites it so urgently that it is rarely, if ever, absent from a test.

The quickest way to understand the virtual inevitability of ambiguity in multiple-choice tests is to try making up a multiple-choice question.

Suppose we try it here. We can even use the above sentence. It is not a very good one, and I am not suggesting that reputable test-makers would be likely to use it. But it is well suited to our present purpose, which is to show how the multiple-choice format exerts its influence on the test-maker. Let us convert the sentence into a multiple-choice question of the sentence-completion type. We merely leave out a word and offer five choices for filling the gap, like this:

The quickest way to understand the .... inevitability of ambiguity in multiple-choice tests is to try making up a multiple-choice question.

    (A) ....
    (B) virtual

(C) ....
(D) ....
(E) ....

That seems simple enough. All we have to do is to think of four words for the wrong choices, A, C, D, and E.

We might try (A) rainy, (C) loving, (D) blonde, (E) cosy. But these words obviously do not fit the sentence at all. They make the question too easy. Besides, as any competent psychologist would quickly realize, they betray that our mind was not on our work: we have been unconsciously making free associations, stimulated by the word *virtual*.

So, back to work. We do not want to make the question trivially obvious. How can we make it difficult? One way is to use relatively obscure words, for example: (A) antiphonal, (C) unifoliate, (D) succinic, (E) refrangible. Now we have a harder question—quite a difficult one, it would seem. Yet a person who knows what these four words mean will find it as simple as before. None of them is in the least relevant. Indeed, even a person who does not know the meanings of these four words may well recognize the word *virtual*, see that it obviously fits, and so take a guess that the others do not.

We had better try again. What we want are relatively well known words that will entice the weaker students away from the wanted answer, *virtual*, by the very plausibility with which they seem to fit into the gap in the sentence. Finding them takes some thought. After a while we may come up with the following: (A) equal, (C) simple, (D) sinister, (E) emotional. Each of these words yields a quite plausible sentence. But none makes as good a sentence as *virtual* does. None is the "best" answer. So at last we have a good multiple-choice question that will discriminate between the good and the bad students.

But have we? What makes us so sure that *virtual* makes the "best" sentence? Could it not be the fact that we have known all along what the sentence actually was? If we look at the sentence less subjectively, with less pride of authorship, trying to forget that the word we deleted was *virtual,* we begin to wonder whether *virtual* really does make the "best" sentence. *Sinister* would change the meaning of the sentence *as we had conceived it,* but it would nevertheless make an excellent sentence (certainly a more powerful one—"the sinister inevitability" is strong stuff), and if a sense of the sinister is what the sentence was meant to convey, a much better one.

The candidate does not know that we had *virtual* in mind. He comes to the questions with no preconceptions as to the intended meaning of the sentence. To him *sinister* may seem particularly apt.

He may also regard *emotional* as a strong candidate. And he may approve the quiet power of the sentence that results from using the word *simple.* As for *equal,* it gives the sentence yet another nuance of meaning, and he must make up his mind whether the fact that the sentence then requires a preceding sentence for its meaning to be complete is a valid reason for rejecting *equal* or not.

In trying to make our question difficult, we have made it ambiguous. Of course, we are just amateurs. But the professionals face the same problem we did. And their solution is too often the same as ours: to create a spurious difficulty by introducing ambiguity. They have an advantage over us. They can try their questions out and look for statistical indications of ambiguity. But these indications are of limited value.

It is not without significance that the professional testers refer to the "wrong" answers as "distractors," "misleads," and "decoys." The decoys are deliberately designed to seem plausible. They are, in fact, deliberate traps. Were they always traps baited with definitely spurious bait one might tolerate them, even though their presence gives the test an air of trickery and deception that is not altogether becoming. But too often the traps are baited unfairly. For it is difficult to draw a sharp line between legitimate wile and illegitimate deceit, and the temptation to trespass on the shadowy no-man's-land between the two is hard to resist. (Harder, even, than the temptation to change metaphors in mid-argument.)

Purely factual questions can be made difficult by merely using obscure, unimportant facts. Making genuinely difficult multiple-choice questions by other means is far from easy, and, under pressure to produce many hard questions, the test-makers tend to succumb to the lure of ambiguity.

How difficult it is to produce a hard multiple-choice question that has precisely one good answer and is free from ambiguity, can be seen from the following question, which was made up by a psychologist as part of a test in a college course in psychology:

A scientific hypothesis must be

> A. true
> B. capable of being proven true
> C. capable of being proven false
> D. none of these

While a psychologist is not necessarily an expert in the art of making up multiple-choice tests, he must be classified as somewhat more than a rank amateur. The above question was designed to test whether the student understood the nature of scientific "proof," the idea being that while experimental verifications of a hypothesis serve to bolster faith in the truth of the hypothesis they can not *prove* the hypothesis true, whereas a single experiment can suffice to prove a hypothesis false. Thus the wanted answer was C. And when we know what is in the tester's mind the question, at first sight, seems quite a good one. Certainly, in this case there was no deliberate attempt to be ambiguous.

When we do not know what the tester had in mind,

though, the question can be puzzling. And if we examine it carefully we find in it all sorts of unsuspected defects.

For example, *mathematical* hypotheses are neither true nor false. They are just hypotheses—axioms on which to build a mathematical structure. Thus neither the wanted answer, C, nor answer A, nor answer B would be valid here, and the best answer would seem to be D. However, one can argue in rebuttal that the phrase "a scientific hypothesis" was not meant to include mathematical ones, any more than it was meant to include purely logical ones. Let us proceed, then, to other difficulties.

We can imagine a scientist accidentally hitting on a true scientific hypothesis. He may not be able to prove it true, but it could be true nonetheless. Such a scientific hypothesis could not be proved false. Thus in this particular case answer C would be incorrect; and the word *must* in the question therefore makes answer C in principle incorrect. Once more we seem to be led to answer D.

Again, we can make hypotheses using perhapsy, telltale words; for example, that *some* objects fall towards the earth. Such a scientific hypothesis can certainly be proved true, and can certainly not be proved false.

Even worse, if we prove a scientific hypothesis false, we automatically prove the negative of the hypothesis true, and the negative is itself a scientific hypothesis. So, because of the word *must,* answer C can not be valid—or so it would seem. Yet "a scientific hypothesis" is ambiguous. Does it mean every scientific hypothesis or just some particular scientific hypothesis? We have automatically been assuming the former. But if we assume the latter, then both answer B and answer C can be justified.

The safest course—though it would actually have led to a zero score on the question—would seem to be to pick answer D. We can, moreover, justify answer D on verbalistic grounds. For no one would deny that a scientific hypothesis *must* be "a scientific hypothesis" and this is neither answer A, nor B, nor C. Therefore it is "none of these."

And yet there is even difficulty with answer D, because of its poor wording. The usual phrasing of such answers is something like "none of the above" or "none of the others." If answer D means this, it is the best answer, though it is not the wanted answer. Even so it is a poor answer, since we have no idea what a scientific hypothesis *must* be—beyond being a scientific hypothesis, this being in fact the deepest justification for answer D that we have given. But what if the phrase "none of these" includes answer D itself, as well it might? Then we have a pretty puzzle. For we can argue that a scientific hypothesis *must* be "none of these" if only because it *must* be a scientific hypothesis, but it can not be D because D is *one* of these. The logic here is not impeccable, but let us leave that to the professional logicians. We have seen, at least, that there can be more to a multiple-choice question than the test-maker imagines, and we can draw two morals, one for the test-maker, whether amateur or professional, and the other for the test-taker. For the former: you can not be too careful about wording—or about choice of answer. And, for the latter, the sort of advice that teachers find themselves having to give to students before they take multiple-choice tests: when in doubt, don't think—just pick.

In discussing the above question we have pushed the argument rather far, for there is no clear line of demarcation between what is cogent and what is not. Here this fact is of small moment. But on a multiple-choice test the decision as to what to regard as cogent can be crucial, making the difference between choosing a wanted answer and choosing an unwanted one. And because test-makers use different standards of cogency, relevance, subtlety, depth, and intellectual rigor in different questions on a multiple-choice test, the candidate can have no reasonable assurance that he is accurately gauging the tester's standard on any particular question.

When told that a particular multiple-choice question is vague or ambiguous, testers sometimes argue that the candidate is expected to recognize the context of the question. In so doing they seem not to realize that they are confirming that the candidate is expected to fathom what is in the tester's mind. Students are well aware that they are expected somehow to do this, though: among themselves they call these tests not "multiple-choice" but "multiple-guess."

Later we shall exhibit other ambiguous questions. Meanwhile, here is unwitting evidence that ambiguity is all too prevalent in multiple-choice tests. On page 631 of the *Fifth Mental Measurements Yearbook,* Harry N. Rivlin, Dean of Teacher Education of the City University of New York, N. Y., reviews some Graduate Record Examinations in Education, these tests having been made by the Educational Testing Service. In the following excerpt from his review Dean Rivlin says kind things about the tests: "Whenever questions deal with judgment rather than facts, there is risk that more than one answer can be defended as the best one. There are remarkably few items in which the key is challengeable."

But note how artlessly revealing are his words "remarkably few" not only of the character of these particular tests, but also of that of multiple-choice tests in general, and of the tolerance of ambiguity that people associated with testing seem to acquire when they do not themselves have to take the tests. What would we infer as to the quality of American college students if an authority praised a first-rate place like Princeton University by saying that it had "remarkably few" illiterate students? Is there not something about Dean Rivlin's statement that recalls that of the character witness who said to the judge "John is sober on Sundays"?

Again, in a booklet *Scholastic Aptitude Test,* published by the College Entrance Examination Board in 1956, describing tests given to students seeking admission to college, and giving sample questions, the following advice is offered on page 18:

As you read through the explanations of the verbal section, you may disagree with what we think to be the correct answer to one or two questions. You may think we are quibbling in making certain distinctions between answer choices. It is true that you will find some close distinctions and just as true that in making close distinctions reasonable people do disagree. Whether or not you disagree on a few questions is not terribly important, however, for the value of the test as a whole is that people who are likely to succeed in college agree in the main on most of the correct answers. It is this that gives the [Scholastic Aptitude Test] its predictive power.

"For this reason, when you find it hard to make or recognize a distinction between answer choices, it is better not to spend much time on that question. It is the whole [Scholastic Aptitude Test] rather than any single question in it that makes the test a good indicator of college ability.

The advice in the last paragraph quoted above has significant implications. Consider it in the light of these mutually exclusive propositions: (a) the test contains genuinely difficult questions that are free from ambiguity but call for reflection and can not be properly analyzed in a short time; and (b) the test is devoid of such questions.

If (b) is true, the advice is reasonable, but the test is unworthy of the highly gifted student since it gives him little if any chance to display his superiority over his merely clever rivals. If (a) were true, the advice would defeat the purpose for which the genuinely difficult questions were included, and would be tantamount to a plea for superficiality despite the presence of these questions. It is difficult to escape the conclusion that the two paragraphs together amount to an admission that genuine depth is not present in the test. What they seem to imply is that the difficult questions are difficult not because they have depth but because they involve close distinctions about which there is room for legitimate doubt; and one may be excused for regarding this as a euphemistic way of confessing ambiguity.

The College Entrance Examination Board seems to have regretted this possibly unintentional admission, for in the 1960 edition of the booklet *Scholastic Aptitude Test* it omits it, and says merely, "Since you will have only a limited amount of time for each section of the test, use your time effectively and work as rapidly as you can without losing accuracy. Do not waste time on questions that are too difficult for you. Go on to the other questions and come back to the difficult ones later, if you have time."

Chapter 5

The "Best" Answer

IT IS APPARENTLY an article of faith among statistical-minded objective testers that they are scientific. A principal reason for this belief of theirs is their manner of handling the problem of deciding which shall be the wanted answers. These testers make two main arguments concerning the wanted answer: one tends to be a plea for vagueness, the other a claim of scientific objectivity. We consider them here in turn.

Rarely do the multiple-choice testers ask the candidate to pick the "correct" answer. Rather, they ask him to pick the "best" answer, or the answer that "best fits," or "is most nearly correct," or the like. This is not unrelated to the ambiguity that haunts the multiple-choice format. In a sense it is a sign of emancipation, a banner proclaiming escape from the true-false trap. But it is sometimes regarded as an excuse for laxity and license. Defenders of multiple-choice tests are apt to use it to condone imprecision and ambiguity. Complain to them, for example, that the wanted answer to a particular question is certainly not a correct one and is not really even a good one, and they will point out that all is well since it is nevertheless "the best."

The testers' argument can seem eminently reasonable when presented abstractly. It has its limitations though, and they must make us wary of accepting it when it does violence to intellectual integrity, as it often does. To see its essential weakness, consider the following multiple-choice question, which, I hasten to mention, was *not* taken from an actual test:

The number of letters in the English alphabet is

(A) 1000   (B) 2000   (C) 3000   (D) 4000   (E) 5089

It is hard to imagine that an intelligent person acquainted with the relevant facts would seriously deny that answer A is "the best." Statistics would confirm the almost complete lack of ambiguity in this question, for practically all the examinees would pick answer A. Despite this, one doubts that any reputable test organization would allow the question to appear on one of its tests—and not merely because it was too "easy."

Here is another "best" answer question:

The number of letters in the English alphabet are

(A) water   (B) fire   (C) air   (D) earth   (E) letters

One recoils in horror. Yet, objectively speaking, this question has its merits. I have actually tried it on various people, and all who deign to answer it agree that E is the "best" answer. Surely such unanimity should not be lightly scorned. Besides, there is excellent reasoning behind the choice of answer E. It goes somewhat as follows: "Any tester foolish enough to make up a question like this would be foolish enough to think E a fine answer; and not even he would be foolish enough to think well of any of the decoys." Moreover, the question is fair, since the bad grammar in the use of the word "are" gives ample warning that precision of thought should not be sought in the question. It is even fairer than we may think, since by suitably interpreting the phrase "the number of letters" as a collective noun, we can palliate the "are" and make quite a plausible case for answer E on its own merits.

This question, by its very extravagance, can tell us important things about testing. For example, it provokes widely different responses. Some people pick answer E with a sense of mild amusement. But a few become highly incensed, and indignantly refuse to pick any answer at all; if told sternly that they *must* pick one, they splutter, grow red in the face, and become emotionally blocked, a fact not without relevance here.

By merely asking for the "best" answer rather than the "correct" answer, the test-maker does not escape his obligation to make good questions. It may be too much to demand of him that each of his multiple-choice questions shall have a correct answer. But we should insist that it at least have a "best" answer that is not only good, but can be shown to be clearly better than the decoys.

But shown to whom? Who shall be the judge? Indeed, in dubious cases who shall decide which answer is the "best"? Your choice of a "best" answer may not coincide with mine. There is not much point in talking about the "best" answer if we do not know what we mean by the term.

There are two schools of thought on this matter. One holds that deciding which is the "best" answer should be done by people expert in the subject of the question. This seems a reasonable idea. But it would be frowned upon by statistically-minded testers. Such testers do not rely on the judgment of subject experts. They would rather decide which is the "best" answer empirically. I can not put the matter better than did Mungo Miller, a psychologist. Dr. Miller wrote to me as follows:

Validity or usefulness of a test question is not determined by the whim of a psychologist but by empirical verification by advance administration to persons known to have or not to have the attribute the test seeks to measure. For example, let us suppose that a psychologist preparing a college aptitude test tries out the question:

> Shakespeare wrote:
>> A. *The Cherry Orchard*
>> B. *King Lear*
>> C. *Pygmalion*
>> D. *Omelet*

Assume further that pretesting establishes that 90% of a very large group of freshmen earning high grades at a wide variety of colleges select answer D, and that 90% of those failing at the same colleges select one of the other three answers, then D is the "right" answer. By putting the finger on likely prospects for success among college applicants the question is serving its purpose. Of course, the answer that will prove to be a "right" one in this sense that really matters, will usually be an answer that is also "right" in the sense of being unambiguously and solely the one that is accepted by experts on the subject matter involved, but this is quite aside from the point and unrelated to the theory of psychological test construction.

This puts the matter clearly and wittily. The argument is revealing—and vulnerable. Therefore, before we discuss it, let us bolster the case of the statistically-minded testers by quoting from a letter written by another psychologist, Marvin S. Beitner. It makes reference to an article of mine in *Harper's Magazine* of which more will be told in later chapters, but the following excerpt from Dr. Beitner's letter is self-explanatory and makes its points with admirable clarity.

Do you propose to "prove" that the judgment of the College Entrance Examination Board is "wrong" and that your own is "right"? Do you imagine that it is somehow "more fair" for a student to guess what is in the minds of "people of commanding intellectual stature" who are *not* psychologists and who are unlearned in test construction? I fear that such a step would lead to a repetition of what you yourself have done —namely to set up personal judgment as the criterion of test item selection and to completely ignore one essential scientific basis of the construction of tests which are used to predict future skill, success, or knowledge: verification through an empirical validation study. The danger of such pitfalls in test construction was recognized many years ago and any well trained psychologist would immediately agree that a multiple-choice test can only make a claim to validity on the basis of a comparison of results of the test with some appropriate external criterion. Thus if the items on a test are arbitrarily written by Professor "A," it cannot be claimed that the test is a scientifically valid screening device for graduate work in physics, (although it *might* be said that it is a valid measure of agreement with Professor "A"). Such a test is completely open to the objections which you make. However, the tests which are considered worthy of the name by psychologists are those which have been appropriately validated empirically. (For example, this might be done by comparing scores on a "management aptitude test" with the actual success (or failure) achieved by a group of management trainees X years later. Then the original test items which distinguish between the factually successful and unsuccessful trainees could be used in the construction of a scientifically sound multiple-choice test with all further argument or debate becoming irrelevant.) Naturally the results of a study such as this would have to be applied to any new group with due consideration of the characteristics of the original research group. (That is, limitations still exist and mistakes can be made if these limitations are not given careful consideration and attention by someone who is well trained in test construction.)

To make the assumption that after such validation one may then go back and criticize specific items of the test as being "wrong," "stupid," or "incorrect," and thereby prove that the test results do not screen trainees as empirically demonstrated, is entirely erroneous. This is dramatically illustrated by the existence of some psychological tests wherein particular items seem to bear no relevance whatever to the ability, trait, or characteristic to be measured. It is sometimes discovered that an item or response which appears to be irrelevant or perhaps even contrary to the desired characteristic, turns out to be one of the best criteria by which to screen subjects. A dramatic illustration of an instance wherein a screening criterion appears to be the complete opposite of what logic dictates occurred in the psychological testing of pilot candidates in the armed forces. It was found that candidates who showed *few* signs of anxiety on tests made poorer pilots than candidates who showed *considerable* evidence of anxiety. One might indignantly protest that this is ridiculous and one might challenge any expert to debate with him the logical issues at stake in pilot selection, maintaining that "good" candidates are *less* anxious than "bad" candidates. This argument is irrelevant to the validity of the test item and it highlights the fact that empirical evidence can demonstrate that "experts" may be very wrong. The post hoc "explanation" or "rationalization" that the "nonanxious" candidates were unable to tolerate anxiety and, therefore, "acted out their impulses" without carefully considering their actions is of no particular relevance to the immediate question at hand, although it may stimulate further research and a deeper understanding of the problem. Similarly in the case of an appropriately validated psychological test your question as to whether a particular item is or is not correct, valid, or logical is irrelevant for the same reason. If the test items were selected because they did in fact discriminate between (eventually) "successful" and "unsuccessful" examinees (by an appropriate criterion) then one is only arguing against an irrefutable fact.

This puts the matter strongly, in a manner that will seem convincing to people who quail before the apparent certainties of science. Scholarship and intellectual integrity must bow before higher authority. Arguing about whether a particular item is correct, valid, or logical is irrelevant— nay, irreverent. It is arguing against an "irrefutable fact," and this hardly sounds like a rational occupation. But arguing *about* it is surely the very essence of science. All our best scientific theories are the result of facing facts. Even the psychologists who tested the pilot candidates did

not fall mute before their unexpected finding. It puzzled
them and they argued over it till they had found a way of
understanding it. However, in the present case the alleged
"irrefutable fact" is an iffy fact at best, depending as it
does on the assumptions that the test items were indeed
selected as stated and that the "appropriate criterion"
was more than just appropriate. Only in the simplest
situations is the criterion of success more than superficially appropriate; and the nature of the discrimination
between "successful" and "unsuccessful" candidates is
statistical, not absolute—a greater percentage of the former candidates than of the latter pick the so-called "best"
answer. Let us discuss the matter of the "best" answer
here from the point of view of the humanist, and content
ourselves with showing that there is an implicit contradiction in the argument of the psychologists. Our initial
point, at first glance, may seem rather trifling. But, as
will be seen, it goes to the heart of the matter. For the
present, then, let us suppose, for the sake of argument,
that no exception can be taken to the statistical manner
in which the test items were selected and validated. Then,
according to Dr. Beitner, that ought to be the end of the
matter. But a glance at the actions of testers themselves
is enough to show that even they believe that there is
more to a test question than just its statistical validity.
For example, the test-makers proofread their tests, and
correct such misprints as *hte* for *the*. Why do they bother
to do so? That such minor misprints would not significantly affect the statistical validity is surely a strong candidate for the status of an "irrefutable fact." Why do the
test-makers themselves ignore it? Is it not because there
are elements in the art of test construction that transcend
mere statistical validity? Except when the testers are testing whether candidates understand the rules of grammar,
they do not write their questions in poor English—deliberately, that is. Infelicity of a minor sort that may have crept

in will not noticeably affect the validation statistics, and correcting it certainly takes time and money. Yet the testers are careful to correct it whenever they notice it.

Let us pursue this further. If the test-makers do not also correct the more serious defects in their questions, such as errors in logic, multiplicity of good answers, and lack of an acceptable answer, they may not properly defend themselves by claiming that they are ruled solely by the validation statistics and that these statistics automatically silence all criticism. For, quite apart from the doubt that would be cast on the validity of the validation statistics if such errors did not affect them significantly, the test-makers would have to explain to a skeptical public why they do nevertheless bother to correct the minor slips and misprints that are of negligible statistical significance. They can not have it both ways. They can not be sensitive to minor misprints and at the same time insensitive to major logical flaws, and then command our respectful silence in the name of statistics and the scientific method.

We shall discuss validation and statistics in more detail in a later chapter. Here we are considering the manner of deciding which is the "best" answer. Both Dr. Miller and Dr. Beitner apparently agree that the decision is to be made statistically, without reference to the wording of the question or the opinions of subject experts: if 90 per cent of the freshmen who earn high grades believe that Shakespeare wrote *Omelet* and not *King Lear,* then the "best" answer will simply have to be *Omelet,* and that is that. Admittedly, Dr. Miller's hypothetical multiple-choice question is a witty exaggeration, but it makes the issue crystal clear. And later we shall discuss sample questions constructed by leading test-makers that will make this *"Omelet"* question seem much less of an exaggeration.

Can we accept the proffered argument? Let us see what it implies. On first looking at tests, we probably had the naive idea that the candidate was required to pick the best answer—not the "best" answer. But we soon realized that he must actually pick the wanted answer, and we may therefore have assumed that his objective was to assess the mental capacity of the test-maker and his advisors so as to pick the answer they would most likely pick. But if we accept the thesis expounded by the two psychologists, the candidate's task is really something different: he must pick the answer he believes most of the best candidates will pick; and mind you, he must pick not the answer he thinks they will honestly believe to be the best, but the answer he thinks they themselves will be guessing that the other best candidates will guess that they themselves will guess.

In this fantastic intellectual merry-go-round, where is there room for depth and intellectual honesty? If the official choice of the "best" answer is made by popular vote of the "best" candidates—and by self-seeking popular vote, at that—how will the truly outstanding candidate fare?

Suppose that, on an actual question, he sees no merit at all in the equivalent of *"Omelet"* and picks the equivalent of *"King Lear,"* while 90 per cent of the "best" candidates honestly believe that the equivalent of *"Omelet"* is both the best answer and the "best" answer. Then he will be counted as "wrong"; and there will be trained psychologists ready to prove him "wrong" scientifically. Indeed, the greater his superiority, the more strongly will the statistics be against him. If he is the only student to pick a *"King Lear"* while 99.9 per cent of the "best" candidates are picking an *"Omelet,"* then, though scholars will applaud him, statistics will damn him overwhelmingly. And test psychologists will too—in the hallowed name of Science. To subscribe blindly to the *"Omelet"* theory of the "best" answer is to condone a wedding of science and democracy that does honor to neither.

A National Merit Scholarship winner at one of our leading universities, who prefers to remain anonymous, has sent me a striking case in point. Through the courtesy of the test publisher, I am able to give the question he mentions exactly as it appeared on the test:

DIRECTIONS: To mark an exercise, first decide which of the four words, if any, is incorrectly spelled. Then find the corresponding row of boxes on the answer sheet, and mark the box corresponding to the misspelled word. If none of the words is misspelled, which is often the case, mark the last box in the row.

98. 1) cartons
2) altogether
3) possibilities
4) intensionally
5) none wrong*

My correspondent wrote to me about this question as follows:

When I reached "intensionally," I frankly was stumped. While the word is a perfectly good word, frequently used in logic and semantics, I knew that the test was for seventh through twelfth graders; if the test-makers intended "intensionally" to be counted as correct, then the question became a test of vocabulary, not spelling ability; if they intended "intensionally" to be counted wrong, then they were denying the word a place in the English language. I marked choice 5. After the test, I found out that the key indicates that "intensionally" is misspelled.

Aside from the simple inaccuracy of Science Research Associates, publishers of the test, it strikes me as unfair to punish a student for knowing too much. The word "intensionally" is frequently used in S. I. Hayakawa's *Language in Thought and Action,* one of the textbooks for the Special Senior English course at . . . School. Most of the Special Senior English class "missed" Question 98, while the remainder correctly guessed that S.R.A. had never heard of "intensionally."

This question points up the weakness of the *"Omelet"*

---

* *The Iowa Tests of Educational Development,* Test 3, Part II, p. 9 (Form X-3S, separate booklet edition). Reprinted by permission of the publisher, Science Research Associates, Inc. This organization officially informs me that "4) intensionally" is designated as the proper choice in the corresponding scoring key.

theory of what constitutes the "best" answer. No test-maker can escape responsibility for what is in his test, or excuse his choice of a "best" answer by hiding behind statistics. If statistics give the seal of approval to an *"Omelet"* or to an assertion that an *"intensionally"* is misspelled, then the test-maker is under a moral obligation —to scholars, if not to test psychologists—to modify the question, or remove it from his test. The test-taker has a right to expect the test-maker to display at least this much intellectual morality; and the conscientious test-maker would, indeed, display it—to the best of his abilities. It is extremely unlikely, for example, that Science Research Associates was aware that its "best" answer was incorrect and nevertheless used "intensionally" intentionally. Thus in the last analysis, statistics or no statistics, the candidate's main task is to gauge the intellectual quality of the test-maker and guess what sort of answer he would be likely to accept as "best."

A two-hour multiple-choice test may contain some two hundred questions, a fact to which professional testers point with pride rather than consternation. In their eyes it is a major selling point, and they speak glowingly of the great efficiency of their tests and the enormous amount of material the tests can cover in a short time.

Let us not fall into the trap. Breadth and efficiency can easily be made to seem admirable. But they are not, in themselves, necessarily desirable, and they can be dearly bought when the price is depth and scope for creativity. Broad coverage without depth can favor the candidate who has superficial knowledge of many things and profound knowledge of nothing. The people who know the most are not always the most valuable people.

In an article in *The New York Times Magazine* on July 30, 1961, Professor Albert Szent-Györgyi, who won the Nobel prize for physiology and medicine in 1937, wrote: "I am often ashamed of my ignorance when meeting colleagues whose knowledge of scientific literature is infinite as compared with mine. But if I am alone, I feel nice in my ignorance. It would weigh me down to know too much. . . . I had several associates who were cleverer than I, but who always left work unfinished, who just played about. I had to part with them, agreeing with Genghis Khan that 'it is the completion which gives value to an action.' This urge toward completion is what must have driven the great artists to write their music, or carve their stone."

Boasts of broad coverage and efficiency hardly prepare us for the tedious repetitiousness of so many multiple-choice tests. A multiple-choice test containing two hundred questions may have broad coverage, but it is not likely to be at all as broad as the large number of questions suggests. There are reasons other than breadth of coverage for having large numbers of questions on these tests. For example, if a multiple-choice tester wants to find out whether a student understands a particular point, he can not do so by means of a single objectively graded multiple-choice question, no matter how small the point may be. The student may pick the wanted answer for a wrong reason, or a different answer for a correct reason. Even if the student does not think at all, he has a 20 per cent chance of picking the wanted answer on a five-choice question by the blind-stabbing technique. Because of all this, the testers tend to cover each point repetitiously by more than one multiple-choice question. They seek safety in numbers.

Even their desire for efficiency leads them to repetitiousness. Consider, for example, verbal analogy questions, these being questions of the type:

Up is to down as fat is to
(A) pig   (B) fire   (C) skin   (D) scrawny   (E) miniscule

From statistical studies, the testers have concluded that, for certain purposes, such questions are efficient

discriminators between "good" and "bad" candidates—
"good" and "bad" being suitably defined. Consequently,
some testers use these verbal analogy questions prodigally
in their tests. They put them in by the dozens, apparently
arguing that the more they have of a good thing the better
—an argument they would hesitate to apply to liquor.

They do the same with other types of multiple-choice
questions that they have reason to regard as efficient.
Indeed, they try out all sorts of multiple-choice questions
to discover by actual experiment which types are statistically the most efficient. Is it not natural for them then
to give up the less efficient types? Why use inefficient types
when efficient ones are available? What if repetitiousness
does result? Will the testers be ready to sacrifice efficiency
just because of that? We can not expect them to do so.
They are doing the best they can with a basically defective
testing instrument. They are trapped by the multiple-
choice format and their own statistical set of values.

We should not be surprised, then, that questions of each
type are apt to appear on multiple-choice tests not singly
but in great clusters. Nor that tedium results. A multiple-
choice test may contain dozens of verbal analogy questions. After them may come dozens of some other type
of questions of comparable efficiency, and then other
dozens of yet other efficient types. And the test itself may
be but one member of a highly efficient test "battery"—
what a felicitously chosen technical term!—going on for
hour after hour after hour after numbing hour.

How genuinely difficult, how worthy of first-rate minds,
can questions be for which answers must be picked at the
rate of one every minute or so, or, in some cases, at the
rate of a hundred an hour? How deeply can such questions
probe and still be machine-gradable? And if the questions
did indeed have depth, how could one reasonably expect
the candidates to give well-considered responses to them
so quickly? Is it likely that the students who can maintain

a lively interest in long successions of small, efficient conundrums are those with deep minds, or even those with an adult set of values?

Let us not sacrifice too much for the sake of efficiency. In some respects a dictatorship is more efficient than a democracy; and a lie detector more efficient and more scientific than a jury. The efficient Nazis made medical experiments directly on men and women. And teachers in America used to teach their pupils the themes of symphonies by fitting the themes with childish words—a method whose efficiency they could demonstrate objectively, and one that would still be widely used had not musicians, parents, and other non-scientific outsiders somehow opened their eyes to the perils of efficiency-worship.

Professor John M. Shlien, of the University of Chicago, a psychologist engaged in counseling, discusses this matter of the efficiency of tests with wisdom and wit in an article, "Mental Testing and Modern Society," that appeared in 1958 in *The Humanist* (published by the American Humanist Association, Yellow Springs, Ohio). Here is what he says:

Tests are sold to us on the basis of their "efficiency." Aside from the validity of this claim, the idea of efficiency itself needs to be re-examined. It is often a short-term concept, and a short-sighted one. Suddenly speaking, the most efficient way to get exactly the proteins you need is to take a bite of the nearest person. To get to the ground floor, jump out the window. But these very immediate goals are not our complete or real ones. Until we have thought about these, we cannot use efficiency, even if it can be delivered. Long-term efficiency may rest much more upon people going where and doing what they want than on placing them where tests say they fit best.

Chapter 6

Better Minds

MULTIPLE-CHOICE TESTS may cover many topics in a short time, and yield machine-made "instant grades" that are not in wholesale disagreement with other, much more laborious estimates of ability extending over several years. But this type of efficiency may be less meritorious than it seems if the multiple-choice tests discriminate against some of the most valuable candidates.

And discriminate they do. Let us not deceive ourselves. There is no question about the existence of this discrimination, though there is some dispute as to the extent of its ramifications. The test-makers themselves admit that their multiple-choice tests of aptitude and achievement do not measure creativity and motivation. They are less ready to concede that these tests penalize depth, subtlety, and critical acumen.

It is obvious from the nature of the tests that they do not give the candidate a significant opportunity to express himself. If he is subtle in his choice of answers it will go against him; and yet there is no other way for him to show any individuality. If he is strong-minded, non-conformist, unusual, original, or creative—as so many of the truly important people are—he must stifle his impulses and conform as best he can to the norms that the multiple-choice testers set up in their unimaginative, scientific way. The more profoundly gifted the candidate is, the more his resentment will rise against the mental strait jacket into which the testers would force his mind. And if, by the questions they use, the testers betray intellectual incompetence, the profound student can hardly escape a feeling of contempt—contempt tinged with dismay that these are the people who have acquired the power to judge him.

As for motivation, what chance has the candidate to show even that he is capable of sustained, probing mental effort when the tests skitter breathlessly from question to question? These tests favor the nimble-witted, quick-reading candidates who form fast superficial judgments. Some of these high-scoring candidates are extraordinarily able, of course; they are the ones who happen to have also at least some of the important attributes that the tests fail to detect. But other high-scoring candidates are meretricious and lack intellectual substance; yet they outscore their betters.

The professional testers would not be much impressed by what has just been written. In their eyes it is unsubstantiated opinion verging on guesswork. They prefer to draw their conclusions from experimental evidence: statistics. But on the issues of creativity and motivation their conclusions are basically the same as those that an intelligent person would infer from the nature of the tests.

The testers were faced with the problem of explaining how it happened that, for example, scores made on College Board tests do not correlate superbly with subsequent college performance. They had to account for the fact that their tests, for all their scientific efficiency, have some remarkable failures: students who score extremely high yet prove dismally disappointing; and students with College Board scores indicative of modest ability who go on to do distinguished work in college. Of course, occasional upsets are inevitable. As the testers hasten to point out, testing is not infallible. But to people who have great faith in the efficacy of the scientific, objective approach to testing, some of the wide discrepancies between what the tests predict and what actually happens can be jolting.

For example, a student took a multiple-choice test for entrance to the Bronx High School of Science, was put on the waiting list, interviewed, and rejected. After spending a year at another school, he reapplied, was accepted, and graduated in the top 10 per cent of his class. He took a multiple-choice test for a New York State Regents Scholarship for college study, but did not receive one. In college, he joined a premedical class of which about half the members had received such Regents scholarships, and though he had an outside job requiring an average of twenty hours a week, he found time for college sports and became an officer of his class; and with all this he graduated first among these premedical students. He was accepted by a leading medical school, and was awarded by his college its most coveted scholarship for students going on to medical school. Yet after taking a multiple-choice test, this time for a New York State Regents Scholarship for medical study, he failed to receive one of these graduate scholarships.

He wrote to me, in June, 1961, as follows: "My feeling about the multiple-choice tests which I have taken . . . is that, as applied to my particular case, they have not been indicative of my ability or capacity to do well in school. I was lucky and things turned out well for me anyway, but I'm sure many others whose abilities were judged primarily on the basis of those tests, were treated unfairly. . . . As opposed to the usual arguments that multiple-choice tests are fallible, I feel that as a method of evaluating ability they are wholly inadequate."

The testers could explain away such cases as this by

saying simply that tests are, after all, not infallible. But, as they realized, that would avoid the central issue. They had to find out *why* the tests were sometimes so strikingly fallible; and they discovered, apparently not without surprise, that the tests did not measure motivation, creativity, and other important ingredients of greatness. Now this, if carefully considered, is seen to be an indictment of the tests. But the testers would prefer to look on it as a sort of exoneration. They suggest that it shows that the tests are actually good, and that in the cases where the tests fail they do so because the student possesses special character traits and other qualities that the tests do not measure and were not designed to measure.

This is a weak excuse, even apart from its hindsight. Imagine what the testers would say of us if we produced a College Entrance test that consisted of pitting the candidates one against the other in games of marbles; and when we were chided because of the rather too frequent failure of our tests to predict which candidates would do well in college, we replied, with simple dignity, that these failures came about because the students possessed traits that our tests did not measure and were not designed to measure.

Suppose we did accept the excuse that multiple-choice tests of aptitude and achievement, such as those given by the College Entrance Examination Board, are not designed to measure motivation and creativity. Could we ignore the charge that such tests favor the superficially brilliant and penalize the student who has depth, subtlety, and critical acumen? Some test-makers try to deny that the tests do this. It strikes too close to home. They can think of no plausible excuse. They can not very well say that the tests were not designed to test depth, subtlety, and critical acumen. Whatever it may be that the tests are supposed to measure, something is seriously wrong if the student with the better mind picks a better answer than the "best" answer chosen by the test-maker aided by all his statistics. To say that the tests are designed to penalize such a candidate would be tantamount to saying that the test is not designed to test deeply what it is designed to test superficially.

Here is a sample question that aptly illustrates the point. It is taken from a booklet, *English Composition,* put out by the College Entrance Examination Board in 1954, describing so-called "English Composition" tests, of which we shall have more to say in a later chapter. In this particular question the candidate is required to choose answer 1 if the underlined part of the sentence is good as it stands, and otherwise to pick the best of the proffered alternatives:

Cod-liver oil is very good for children. It gives them vitamins they might otherwise not get.

(1) NO CHANGE   (2) , it
(3) , for it   (4) ; for it

According to the College Board, the question is "easy." Yet competent candidates would have difficulty deciding between answers 1 and 3. I have consulted professors of English, and they agree that either of these answers is acceptable. At first sight, then, the question appears to be ambiguous. But it is actually worse than ambiguous.

In real life the choice between answers 1 and 3 might depend on the rhythm of the context. If long, involved sentences surrounded the given passage, that might be a good reason for breaking it into two short sentences. If it came in the midst of a sequence of short sentences, it might be better as a single sentence than as two.

In the absence of any context, the average student would be inclined to flip a coin. He would have a 50 per cent chance of picking the wanted answer by this method.

The pedant, who happened to know some special rule of grammar or punctuation that seemed appropriate, would doubtless apply it routinely. He too would have a 50 per cent chance of picking the wanted answer.

The deep student encountering the question on a test and not knowing that it was "easy"—how shocked he would be to be told!—would seek internal clues that would lead to an intelligent choice. And he would find two powerful clues.

In the first place, the sentence reads ". . . vitamins they might otherwise not get," not ". . . vitamins *that* they might otherwise not get." Clearly the style is laconic. Not for it the measured formality of ", for it." The forthright ". It" has the proper tone. And, in the second place, if corroborative evidence is needed that answer 1 is preferable to answer 3, it is found in the forthright word "get." Would not a writer who used the more formal ", for it" be more likely to use "obtain"? Reasoning thus, the deep student would pick answer 1, with a feeling of delight at the charming subtlety of the question. And, fortunately for his peace of mind, he would probably never learn that he had scored zero on it. But imagine how he would feel on encountering the question in a booklet describing the College Board's so-called "English Composition" tests and learning that the wanted answer is in fact not 1 but 3.

One of the reasons there is not a greater outcry against current multiple-choice tests is precisely that the better candidates rarely discover that their subtle probings have led them to pick better answers than they were supposed to.

Sometimes the deep student can see at once that the tester was inept. For example, a student told me of a question he had to answer on a test, made by one of the five leading test publishers, that was basically as follows:

Each of the boys gave ‑‑‑‑‑‑‑‑‑ oath
(A) his   (B) their

The average person who knows the rules of grammar will realize that "each" is singular and so pick answer A, scorning answer B as a trap for dullards and nincompoops. But the deeper person will realize that the question is utterly ambiguous. If each of the boys gave his individual, personal oath, then A is correct. But suppose, for example, there was a troop of Boy Scouts that had a special oath. Then, whether "each of the boys" in the question belonged to the troop or not, he could give the troop's oath. And if the intent of the sentence was to emphasize the corporate nature of this oath, answer A would be wrong and answer B correct.

A correspondent sent me a similar example, again a question encountered on an important test made by one of the five leading test-makers. In this question the candidate must pick the one word, *if any,* that makes the sentence incorrect. The sentence reads somewhat as follows:

Among them, Tom and Dick were not able to find enough money. . . .

The average student who knows the rules of grammar will doubtless pick the word "among" because, when only two people are involved, the appropriate word is "between."

But the deeper student will read less hastily and realize that the word "them" in the sentence is indefinite in its implications. It might refer to Tom and Dick, in which case picking "among" would be correct. But it might refer instead to a larger group, of which Tom and Dick were the financial custodians; or even to a group that Tom and Dick were robbing at gun-point. If so, the sentence would be correct as it stood, and picking "among" would be wrong. The question is ambiguous. But only the deeper students are likely to realize this, and only they are likely to be disturbed by it. Clearly, then, the question penalizes the deeper students, and does so even if they pick the wanted answer.

In the last two cases above, the deep students might

well answer "correctly," realizing that the tester was probably unaware of the ambiguities and making allowances for his shortcomings, thereby confirming the tester in his belief that his statistics showed that the questions were sound and that the best students picked the wanted answers because of the merits of those answers rather than because they recognized the deficiencies of the tester.

But it is not always clear what the tester has in mind, or what his statistics will tell him. The "oath" question and the "money" question above came to my attention not just because deep students saw more in them than the test-makers and their expert committees could see, but because in seeing more they realized that the questions were ambiguous and thus defective. Not all defective questions flash such warning signals. How many current test questions may there not be that lead the deeper students astray without their ever realizing it?

When a deep student, for excellent reasons, picks an unwanted answer, it is obvious that he suffers the penalty of a zero score on the question. But when he ends by picking the wanted answer, the testers would have us believe that he suffers no significant penalty. They ignore what was pointed out in Chapter 1 in connection with the *"Emperor"* and "colonies" questions: that he has had to expend more time and mental energy than his more superficial competitors did, and that, if the question was visibly defective, he has learned to doubt the competence of the test-maker and thus to look with suspicion on other questions, no matter how innocent they may seem. The testers are sometimes scornfully dubious—we shall give an instance in a later chapter—of the effect on the test-taker of this doubt of the test-maker's competence. Yet basically it is the halo effect (see page 46), the very effect they cite so eagerly as an argument in favor of objective grading.

The doubt can be most upsetting. Imagine a sensitive,

intelligent job-seeker sitting nervously, hat in hand, on the edge of his chair. As the curtain rises on this scene the Great Man addresses the job-seeker in a kindly tone:

"I'm the examiner here. I make up the questions and I grade them."

"Yes, sir."

"You don't need to be nervous."

"No, sir."

"All you do is answer some questions."

"Yes, sir."

"They're not hard. You'll probably find them easy. But they tell me a lot of stuff about you."

"Yes, sir."

"O.K. First I test your English. All set? Just answer yes or no, and don't give me no arguments."

The curtain falls as the test goes inexorably on.

It is not the presence of defective questions that makes multiple-choice tests bad. Such questions merely make them worse. Even if all questions were impeccable, the deep student would still be at a disadvantage. He would see more in a question than his more superficial competitors would ever dream was in it, and would expend more time and mental energy than they in answering it. That is the way his mind works. That is, indeed, his special merit. But the multiple-choice tests are concerned solely with the candidate's choice of answer, and not with his reasons for his choice. Thus they ignore that elusive yet crucial thing we call quality.

Suppose, for example, that we ask the mailman whether it will rain today, and he says "Yes." And then we ask an expert at the weather bureau and he too says "Yes." They may both turn out to be wrong. Yet the meteorologist's "yes" was of much higher quality than the mailman's, though a statistically-minded, objective, multiple-choice grader might be aghast at hearing us say so.

Do not think that the tests discriminate against the

deep candidates only when the candidates are old enough to be capable of sophisticated argument. Younger people are given simpler tests, yet even so the problem is present. Professor Durrett Wagner, of Kendall College, wrote me that, in a lesson on health in a first-grade class, his son was given two drawings, one suggesting a wide-awake, lively child and the other a drowsy one, and was told to circle the figure that indicated what he is like when he gets up in the morning. Wrote Professor Wagner, "He brought home the booklet made in school for me to look at; when we got to page 12, he said to me: 'You know why I drew a line just halfway around each figure, Daddy?' Unimaginative as I am, I did not. 'Well, because when *I* wake up in the mornings, I am half happy and half droopy.' "

Again, a school principal, Leonard Vogel, brought to my attention the following letter which he received from Mrs. A. Bernstein, a teacher in his school:

While administering the New York Inventory of Mathematical Concepts for Grade 1 I observed what I consider to be an interesting and pertinent reaction to this test. Some of my brightest children hesitated longest before marking their answers. They also sought to establish more facts than the original question provided. It occurred to me that perhaps these children brought so much knowledge to the test that they were actually being penalized. Rather than accepting the questions at "face" value these children were seeking greater depth and meaning than the questions required.

I have brought this to your attention because I thought it might be of interest and some value in the research and development of any future tests.

With regard to the age associated with college admission, it is instructive to quote from an article, by Professor J. W. Getzels of the University of Chicago, entitled "Non-IQ Intellectual and Other Factors in College Admission." It was part of a symposium on "The Coming Crisis in the

Selection of Students for College Entrance" held in 1960 under the auspices of the American Educational Research Association, a department of the National Education Association.

In his article, as Professor Getzels explains, he deliberately overstates the case somewhat, in order to raise the argument and sharpen the issues. Speaking of achievement tests, aptitude tests, school recommendations, and high school ranks based on teacher grades, he says that "these indices favor the student who is retentive and docile—the one who tends to seek the single pre-determined, 'correct' answer to an intellectual problem—as against the student who is constructive and creative—the one who tends to seek the multiple, experimental, 'novel' answer to an intellectual problem. . . . Imagine then my surprise to discover that the vast preponderance of problems on current college selection tests are of the multiple-choice variety prohibiting the possibility of the creative kind of formulation but requiring only that the student be able to match his solution to a pre-determined single correct and sometimes quite pedestrian answer. Under these test conditions, which demand only skill in picking commonly accepted responses to questions—conditions, if one stops to think of it, that in many cases do not demand even recall, to say nothing of intellectual construction or creation, but only recognition—the student . . . with a preference for the pre-determined solution, is clearly at an advantage. . . ."

Chapter 7

"What's in a name?"

TESTING IS no game. It is in deadly earnest. If tests are misused, the consequences can be far from trifling. Lives can be warped and careers ruined—as much by unwarranted promotions as by misguided guidance and lack of recognition of ability. The zest and creativity of a business organization may be dampened and destroyed. The strength and vitality of a nation may be jeopardized.

Tests are misused when they are taken too seriously. Though testing is no game, people in positions of responsibility would do well to treat it as one. Otherwise professional judgment becomes overawed and atrophied, and professional testers take over.

In England, testing is still regarded more as an art than a science. The examiners are apt to be scholars rather than professional testers, and tests are seldom of the multiple-choice variety. Yet even in England, a country not usually given to going to extremes, important people have evidently let themselves be taken in by exaggerated claims about the efficacy of testing. How else can one account for the "eleven plus" examinations? For almost twenty years these have been given to school children at a tender age—between ten and one-half and eleven and one-half—

so that the authorities can decide their futures by saying with an air of assurance that this child is worthy of a higher education and that one is not. Able Englishmen who have achieved distinction have expressed deep bitterness at having been effectively denied a chance at a university education because they failed their "eleven pluses" and were forthwith placed in classes that were given manual training and intellectual pap.

Fortunately there is a rising sense of outrage and revolt in England against the "eleven plus" examinations; but how could responsible adults have brought themselves to take tests so seriously in the first place, especially tests given at so early an age?

One of the minor reasons that tests are taken so seriously is that people are confused by the strategical misuse of language. As an example, consider the "reading readiness" tests. The name, "reading readiness," seems reasonable. Yet it is misleading. These tests are given to children around the age of six, ostensibly so that teachers can determine which of the children are "ready" to start to learn to read. But actually they are given so that teachers can determine which children are *not* yet ready even at this late age. The tests are not "reading readiness" tests but "reading unreadiness" tests. This is no quibble. If they were really "reading readiness" tests, they would be given initially at a much earlier age, so that as soon as a child became "ready" for reading his readiness would be detected and he could be started on reading right away.

Even if the tests were so used, it is questionable whether the name "reading readiness" would be justified. Here is what Professor John B. Carroll, of Harvard University, has to say on the subject in an article, "Research in Education: Where Do We Stand?" in the Winter, 1960, issue of the *Harvard Graduate School of Education Association Bulletin*:

Let's consider one of the better [reading readiness] tests and one of the problems connected with it. Mr. [James B.] Conant is very much interested in the problem of reading, so I have tried to discover what we could find out about reading tests, beginning with reading readiness tests. I tried to find the most practicable and best validated one. A search through Buros [i.e. the Mental Measurements Yearbooks, which he edits] and through various testing handbooks, reading textbooks, and other sources, failed to turn up anything that really satisfied me. There wasn't a single reading readiness test which would pass muster on most of the customary criteria, such as adequate validity, reliability, and standardization. And yet these reading readiness tests are being very widely used. I took one that seemed to be pretty good, the Lee-Clarke Reading Readiness Test, and looked in the manual that goes with it.

One of the things this test is supposed to do is to tell you how much one should delay the start of formal instruction in reading. That is, if the child gets a score of such and such, you can start him reading at the beginning of the first grade. If he gets a score below that, you're supposed to delay him three to six months, and so on. This is an interesting claim, and I tried to see whether we have any research evidence to justify it. A diligent search failed to disclose in the test manual, or in any of the writings of the test's authors, any research evidence which would justify the delay of reading work on the basis of scores on the test. The only kind of validity offered was the correlation between test scores and reading success at the end of the first year. Some of these correlations were quite good, .60 or thereabouts. But that still does not justify using the test as a basis for delaying children in reading work. I would challenge you to find anything in the literature that relates to this problem.

And later Professor Carroll remarks that the sociologist O. K. Moore has demonstrated that "it is possible to teach children to read at the age of two-and-a-half years."

It may seem a small matter that these tests are called

"reading readiness" tests rather than "reading unreadiness" tests. Yet "reading readiness" tends to obscure the true purpose of the tests. When impatient parents wonder why their bright children are not being taught to read, and the school principal tells them they must wait till their children pass the "reading readiness" test, the parents are apt to feel that this is a reasonable rejoinder. What would they think if they were told they must wait till their children were deemed old enough to take the "reading unreadiness" test? And, more important, what would they do? A strategically chosen title like "reading readiness" can prevent the building up of pressures for reform. Imagine what might happen if the curious significance of "readiness," pointed out by Professor Carroll, were to become widely known among parents whose children had been held back from reading because they had been objectively rated "not ready."

"Objectively," of course, is another strategically chosen word to be wary of, as we have already seen.

Then there are "underachiever" and "overachiever." These are sheer propaganda words. If, for example, a student scores well on IQ tests but does badly in schoolwork, he is called an "underachiever." And if he scores badly on the tests but does well in school he is called an "overachiever," a word that may startle us with its self-contradictory implication that a person can somehow achieve more than he is capable of.

The vice of these words, "underachiever" and "overachiever," is that they all too often treat the tests as the standards: if the tests say the student is able, then able he is, no matter what his teachers think; and if the tests say he is not, nothing he does will make him otherwise. Professional testers and their more naive clients see nothing amiss in the choice of the words "underachiever" and "overachiever." It would not occur to them to place more credence in the teachers' collective judgments of actual performance than in the scores on the tests, to the extent of calling the academic "underachiever" an "overscorer" on tests and the "overachiever" an "underscorer."

We may not dismiss the words "underachiever" and "overachiever" as just subtle propaganda that does no serious harm. School principals and counselors are too often taken in by them. It is understandable that parents of "overscorers" who are told that their children are "underachievers" should be unhappy about the actual performance of their children. And it is equally understandable that parents of "underscorers" who are told that their children are "overachievers" should be dismayed at the label even though they are not depressed about the abilities of their children. But it is not understandable that some school officials should look askance at the "overachievers," mistrust their demonstrated ability, and fail to place them in accelerated classes; and, as occasionally happens, should feel an urge to try to correct the "overachievers' " seeming aberration of doing better than they were supposed to.

At a PTA meeting an expert on testing, to my surprise, began his talk by saying "All group tests stink." But as the talk progressed one began to realize that this opening statement had been merely a device to disarm criticism. By the end of his talk the expert was saying that if a teacher's estimate of a student's ability conflicted with the rating given by tests—he was talking of the well-known Iowa Tests at the time—then the teacher was wrong. At least, he made the transition gently. It took him the better part of an hour to go from his opening remark to his conclusion. Greater haste might have had disastrous effects on the good will of his audience.

One of the most serious misuses of words by testers is connected with the *iquination quotient,* or IQ, which they refer to as the *intelligence quotient.* A person's *iquination* is measured by his score on an IQ test in relation to his age; and iquination itself is that quality, attribute, capability, or potentiality that is measured by his score on an IQ test in relation to his age. While this may sound like a circular definition it is, as psychological definitions go, precise, objective, and scientific, even though different IQ tests yield different IQ's.

Originally, IQ tests were indeed called *intelligence tests,* but this specialized use of the loose, popular word "intelligence" proved confusing. People who considered themselves intelligent thought they knew, at least approximately, what they meant when they used the word "intelligence" intelligently, and they wondered whether the intelligence testers were measuring the sort of thing the word "intelligence" suggested. There was considerable technical discussion of the point among psychologists, and ultimately intelligence testers took refuge in the above operational definition that *intelligence* is that which is measured by means of intelligence tests. This put them in a strong position. They could no longer be accused of measuring something other than intelligence as thus defined, yet they could still reap the benefits of the connotations of the word "intelligence" in its original, non-technical sense. They persisted, for example, in the custom of referring to students with extremely high IQ's as geniuses, though they knew very well that genius is not significantly related to extremely high intelligence in the ordinary sense of the word nor to extremely high intelligence in the testers' sense of the word. To allow a word like "genius"—to say nothing of "intelligence"—to be polluted and bastardized in this way is hardly becoming conduct on the part of testers.

Psychologists now generally agree that the IQ does not measure an innate, fixed, untrained ability of the sort that ordinary people have in mind when they use the word "intelligence." Indeed, so badly has the word been damaged by its misuse in connection with IQ's, that psychologists who seek to measure certain important aspects of intellectual power find themselves in the awkward position of having to refer to them technically as "non-intelligence intellectual characteristics."

When psychologists themselves are inconvenienced by the strategic misuse of a word, matters have really gone too far. Because of the unfortunate confusion caused by the misuse of "intelligence" in connection with IQ's, the new technical term *iquination* was proposed.* By its freedom from everyday connotations, it contributes greatly to clarity and precision of thought. To see how it does this, compare these two ways of referring to a child who makes a low score for his age on a group IQ test: "He has low iquination," and "He has low intelligence." The former has no irrelevant overtones. But even if we are fully aware of the narrow and transitory significance of the IQ and how tenuously it is related to what we usually think of as intelligence, can we wholly escape the misleading implications of the latter phrase? Does it not seem somehow to brand the child?

Again, there is little temptation to refer to a student with an extremely high iquination quotient as a genius; and if someone did refer to him as a genius the irrelevance of the word would be manifest. If Edison was correct when he said that genius is one per cent inspiration and 99 per cent perspiration, then iquination tests would be 100 per cent unrelated to genius, for they measure neither the amount of the one nor that of the other.

Belief that iquination tests measure innate intelligence can have grave consequences. Such things as the injustices done to "underscorers" are obvious. What is less well understood is that more massive evils can flow from this misconception of the nature of the IQ. In the New York City school system there is a highly successful *Higher Horizons* program. At certain schools in underprivileged

* It was proposed in 1962, by Banesh Hoffmann; see *The Tyranny of Testing*, Crowell-Collier Press, p. 109.

neighborhoods an all-out effort was made to interest the students in cultural matters, to improve their English—some of the students came from homes where a different language was spoken—and to give the students an enthusiasm for the idea of going to college.

In the planning stage the idea of such a program met with considerable resistance. Why? Because, even though the Educational Testing Service was one of the important backers of the idea, there were people who insisted that the average IQ in these schools was so low that the experiment was foredoomed to failure and that any efforts expended on trying to engage the interest of the students and give them an enthusiasm for higher education would be a waste of time and energy, not to mention the taxpayers' money. These people thought that an IQ measures not iquination but intelligence; in their view a low IQ was a low IQ, and that was that.

Fortunately, wiser heads prevailed and a pilot experiment was made. The IQ's of underprivileged children tend to decrease in successive years. But in an experimental group of 105 students, the average IQ was increased from 95 to 102.7. In three years, the average IQ of the 49 boys in the group changing from 91.4 to 104.2, a gain of nearly 13 points. One student gained 40 points, and 40 students gained more than 10 points while only 6 students lost more than 10 points, one of the latter losing 31 points. In a later experimental group of 81 students, there were comparable increases in the average IQ's, and while 3 students lost from 6 to 10 points and 1 student lost from 10 to 15 points, 5 students gained from 31 to 40 points, 1 student gained from 41 to 50 points, and 2 students actually gained from 51 to 60 points.

It is clear from this that iquination is not the same as what we usually think of as intelligence. Defenders of IQ's may object that we are not here discussing a normal situation, pointing out that these students received very special attention for up to three years, and that probably language difficulties were, at least in part, the cause of their poor early showing. But would not this argument in fact emphasize that these particular IQ tests were not measuring intelligence?

And would it not make even more startling those *losses* ranging up to 31 points?

In 1959, the American Association of School Administrators, the Council of Chief State School Officers, and the National Association of Secondary-School Principals set up a joint committee to study testing at the secondary-school level. In 1962 the committee issued a strongly-worded report, *Testing, Testing, Testing,* that had this to say, in part, about the IQ: "Often the first question asked about a pupil by a teacher is, 'What's his IQ?' And the answer, regardless of its accuracy, often determines the posture of some, if not all, of his teachers toward him. This practice continues despite the innumerable examples of frightfully inaccurate IQ scores."

It would be unfair to leave the impression that responsible test experts are unaware of the limitations of the IQ. On the contrary, they are often sharply outspoken about these limitations, stressing how untrustworthy the IQ is even in normal situations, and how utterly misleading it can be in the case of culturally deprived children, especially when their native language is not that of the test. One would imagine that these strictures would long since have impressed all officials whose duties require them to use IQ's. But the long-continued propaganda in favor of the IQ, and the insidious effect of the phrase "intelligence quotient" cause some of these people to behave as though they were completely lacking in—well, in intelligence. In a school in one of the largest cities in the United States, a young girl had been doing very nicely in slow regular classes in the third, fourth, and fifth grade with three successive teachers. In the fifth grade she was at the top of her class. Yet the school psychologist, discovering that the student's IQ was below 70, had her taken out of the class in which she was doing so well and placed in a class for mentally retarded children. Nor is this all. When the fifth-grade teacher complained, the assistant principal told her that performance did not count—only the IQ counted. Nor is even this all. The teacher brought the matter to the attention of leading figures in the world of testing and received virtually unanimous letters strongly condemning the action of the school psychologist in ignoring actual school performance and relying instead on the IQ, especially since the girl's native language was not English—a fact of which the school psychologist was well aware. The teacher showed these powerful letters to the school principal, and the principal agreed that the student had done very well in her regular fifth-year class—but he backed the psychologist. And he in turn was backed by higher authorities.

There has recently been much discussion of the advisability of letting parents know their children's IQ's. One begins to wonder whether the discussion ought not instead to have been directed at the advisability of letting this information fall into the hands of school psychologists and school principals.

More striking than the misuse of the word "intelligence," is the extraordinary use to which responsible and highly respected testers have put the phrase "English composition."

To anyone who does not comprehend how the mind of a dedicated tester works, the story may seem incredible. The organizations involved are the College Entrance Examination Board and the Educational Testing Service, the latter making and scoring the tests given by the former.

Between them, these two organizations had found what

they regarded as a reasonably satisfactory solution to the problem of discovering, by means of tests, which students were likely to do well in college. They had devised the *Scholastic Aptitude Test.* In a general way, this multiple-choice test was akin to an iquination test; but it had two separate parts—a verbal part and an arithmetical part—and could thus yield two distinct scores for each candidate. In this respect it was a marked improvement over the usual iquination test, which gave each candidate a single combination score that was said to measure his intelligence.

In 1956, in the *College Board Review,* a Board committee, reporting on a different matter, spoke, in this connection, of "the single misleading and uninformative IQ which was used for many years as a reliably valid measurement"—a comment that acquires an ironical aspect when we realize that IQ tests are still extensively used and much revered, and that many people are under the impression that the "scientific" evidence in favor of the IQ tests is compelling.

At least, the makers of the *Scholastic Aptitude Test* recognized that aptitude has more than one facet. Why was it called the *Scholastic Aptitude Test?* Partly as a protest against the misuse of the word "intelligence." And, more specifically, because it was used for measuring the likelihood of a candidate's doing well in college, and was validated by comparing scores on the test with subsequent, as well as current, college grades. But if one looked at the test one came away with the impression that college aptitude consists, first, of an ability to answer rather trifling though sometimes tricky arithmetical, algebraic, and geometrical multiple-choice questions and, second, of an ability to pick synonyms and antonyms, to complete verbal analogies, to select words that "best" fill gaps in sentences, and to read prose passages and pick "best" answers relating to them.

In addition to testing this "scholastic aptitude," the Board wished to test for achievement in specific subjects. Here, too, it preferred to test by multiple-choice methods. Let us not suppose, though, that the Board is unalterably opposed to essay tests. It is beset by many pressures and follows a zigzag path. Take the Advanced Placement program, for example. This important program, fostered by an agency of the Ford Foundation, allows superior students to do college work in high school without having to repeat it in college. Naturally, a student must know the work well before a college will allow him to skip a college course in it. The Advanced Placement program had to be acceptable not just to college committees on admissions but to departmental chairmen. It might never have been accepted by the chairmen had it been based on multiple-choice tests only. So candidates for advanced placement are given tests consisting of a multiple-choice part and a longer, essay part. Both parts are graded for the Board by the Educational Testing Service; and the graded essay parts are sent to the appropriate departmental chairmen so that they can see for themselves whether they agree with the grades assigned.

In the case of regular college entrance achievement tests, though, the College Board preferred to confine itself to multiple-choice tests, even in such subjects as foreign languages. But one subject caused it unusual concern: English composition. For here objective techniques seemed particularly irrelevant. To see if a student is good at English composition, we might think it appropriate to have him write English compositions, preferably on various occasions. But that would mean giving essay questions. The College Board and the Educational Testing Service had had long experience with essay questions, and knew their faults all too well. They decided, therefore, to try more modern techniques; to try, in fact, to assess ability in English composition objectively. The first step in this scientific undertaking was to list attributes and abilities needed in order to write a good English composition: the ability to punctuate, to choose the appropriate word, to place ideas in logical order, to recognize and rectify grammatical error and incorrect usage, to sense whether a particular style is appropriate, and so on.

Now came the dazzling—though, to a tester, routine—idea of testing each one of these fractionalized attributes individually, mainly by multiple-choice questions, and then lumping the individual scores into a single composite score measuring the candidate's ability at English composition.

Having constructed a synthetic test along these lines, the Educational Testing Service, naturally, called it the *English Composition Test*. A miracle had been performed. Ability at English composition could now be tested effectively, efficiently, and scientifically by means of a synthetic *English Composition Test* without the candidate being put to the inconvenience of writing an English composition—or the tester of grading it.

Of course, there was an outcry against this novel concept from teachers who heard of it. And from some professional testers too. For instance, in a review of these *English Composition Tests* in the *Fourth Mental Measurements Yearbook*, Professor Frederick B. Davis and Charlotte Croon Davis, both professional testers, having studied the tests in detail and being apparently unaware of the outcry against them, wrote: "If the rank and file of teachers of college-preparatory English could have the same opportunity as the reviewers to study these examinations, it is hard to believe that a chorus of disapproval would not arise."

Criticism was stilled for a while by means of statistics. But it could not be suppressed completely, even within the College Board itself. Largely because of the inspired persistence of Dr. Earle G. Eley, then an examiner at the

University of Chicago, the Board found it expedient to reintroduce a genuine English composition test on an experimental basis, hoping thereby to convince the skeptics once and for all that its synthetic tests were superior.

The experiment lasted three years, from 1954 to 1957, the new essay test being called the *General Composition Test* to emphasize that the essay topics were not purely literary. The experiment was an elaborate one and we give here only its bare outline. Students were given not only the new essay test, but also the *Scholastic Aptitude Test* and the synthetic *English Composition Test*. The essays in the *General Composition Test* were graded by experienced teachers and professors of English under carefully controlled conditions, with much consultation and comparison to ensure maximum uniformity of standards. Two people independently read each paper, and if they gave conflicting grades a third reader was called in.

There remained the problem of discovering which students really were the good ones at English composition, and which the bad ones. This was, of course, the crux of the matter. Without a standard, it was impossible to decide which of the three tests gave the most accurate grades. So, before the students took the *General Composition Test,* the College Board and the Educational Testing Service asked teachers of English composition at selected schools to rate their students on the basis of many essays each student had written in school. Naturally, the graders of the *General Composition Test* were not told the ratings that the teachers had made of their students.

The teachers' ratings were the standard. How did the three types of test fare when measured against it?

The *General Composition Test* came out worst. The *English Composition Test,* which contained no essays, gave better agreement with the teachers' ratings, and did so with only one hour of examination time as against the two hours of the *General Composition Test*. As for the

Scholastic Aptitude Test, its ninety-minute verbal part, which had not been intended as a test of English composition at all, turned out to be the best of the three.

Here was powerful evidence with which to confound the doubters. And there was more, as the professional testers had confidently expected there would be: for example, disagreements among the essay graders about the merits of the same essay, and the finding that students who took the tests in two consecutive years tended to receive disparate ratings on the *General Composition Tests* but relatively consistent ratings on the non-essay tests. Taking all such things into account, and noting the high cost of grading essays, the College Board voted to discontinue the experimental essay test and to revert to the synthetic, non-essay *English Composition Test.*

This all sounds so reasonable, so logical, and so scientifically conclusive. Yet if we are scholars our instincts rebel. Every step in the argument seems irrefutable. Yet the result feels all wrong. Why? What is awry in this pretty picture?

Well, for one thing, it lacks self-consistency. I remember once complaining about an ROTC band that was allowed to practice while marching up and down outside a classroom in which I noticed that a multiple-choice examination was being held. The band would not be shushed, nor could I get it removed to a more distant place. And when I persisted in my complaints a psychologist told me that I was making an unnecessary fuss since on other occasions when candidates had been disturbed by similar outside noises, they had actually tended to score higher, the distractions evidently causing them to concentrate all the harder. I was nonplussed. One can not argue effectively against assertions of experts by merely raising one's eyebrows, especially when what the experts say may well be true. But after a minute or so it occurred to me to test the psychologist by pushing the argument to its logical conclusion. I suggested that we ought to have a special college fund to pay for hiring bands to rehearse while tests were being taken, since that would help the students concentrate and raise their scores. When the psychologist looked at me as if I were a lunatic, I realized that the expert assertion about the beneficial effect of distraction had been just a professional attempt to confound me, and need not be taken seriously—except, perhaps, insofar as it might reflect on the manner in which psychologists deal with people who are not professional psychologists.

Let us examine the action of the College Board in the matter of the non-essay *English Composition Test*. The principal reason for preferring this test to the *General Composition Test,* which was an essay test, was that the former had been clearly demonstrated to provide better measurement of ability at English composition than the essay test did. That was the argument used by the College Board to confound the skeptics. If the skeptics were supposed to accept the argument, then they in turn had a right to expect the College Board to believe in it too. But the College Board continued to use the synthetic, non-essay *English Composition Test*. Why? Was it because that test had been scientifically proved superior to the essay test as a measurer of ability in English composition? If that was the reason, why did the Board not use the verbal part of the *Scholastic Aptitude Test* instead? Had that not been proved, in the very same way, to be superior to the *English Composition Test* for this very purpose?

It would be a simple matter—at least for the College Board and the Educational Testing Service—to give an appropriate new name to the verbal part of the *Scholastic Aptitude Test,* with its synonyms, antonyms, analogies, sentence completions, and paragraph comprehension questions. They could, for example, call it the *New and Improved English Composition Test*. The name would be amply justified on objective scientific grounds, except, perhaps, for the word "new," and even that could be defended. The test was demonstrably superior to the *English Composition Test*—with its "objective" questions on such things as grammar, style, and the ordering of ideas—which, in turn, was demonstrably superior to the essay test. And imagine the efficiency and economy inherent in the *New and Improved English Composition Test*: it could be given simultaneously with the verbal part of the *Scholastic Aptitude Test,* and the amount of extra grading needed could be truly described as negligible.

Why did the College Board retain the synthetic *English Composition Test,* and not replace it by the new and improved model? The former had been constructed allegedly as a test of English composition, but the latter had clearly not been. Was it this that made the College Board stop short? Was the Board fearful that by going over to the new and improved Scholastic Aptitude model it would make all too plain that neither the new nor the old was in fact a test of English composition? As Spencer Brown pointed out, in another connection, in an article in the June, 1959, issue of *Commentary,* "there is a high correlation in high school seniors between knowledge of trigonometry and knowledge of physics. But if the physics teacher marks his students on the basis of a test in trigonometry, [objectors] will remind him of the validity of content, even if they do not use the term."

Despite their scientific claims and their semantic antics, the College Board and the Educational Testing Service do not test English composition with their *English Composition Test.* If we believe they do, we delude ourselves. They test things related to English composition, but these are more the piecemeal attributes of the grammarian and the critic than of the creative writer or even the gifted expositor. And, because they test each attribute singly, and not in combination with the others, they test even these things badly. The ability to walk, for example, is not the ability to make various primary body movements separately but the ability to perform them in proper coordination, and even with a certain nonchalance. Nor is the best walker necessarily the one who best performs the constituent motions separately.

What would we think of a publishing house that mistrusted editorial judgment and decided which manuscripts to publish by subjecting their authors to a verbal aptitude test, or to the College Board's synthetic *English Composition Test*? Even if the method brought increased income, would we wholly approve? What would we think of the Metropolitan Opera if, when auditioning singers, it objectively tested first their posture, then their technique of breathing, then their understanding of musical notation, then their sense of rhythm, then their eyesight (the conductors would insist on that), then their ability to recognize whether a note was on pitch, then their ability to recognize what was wrong in various specimens of deliberately faulty singing previously recorded on tape, and finally, the quality of each individual tone of the voice, note by note, from the lowest to the highest—but did not ask for an aria because examiners too often disagreed in rating such a complex thing?

The College Board's experiment was supposed to have demonstrated that, of the three tests, the essay test was the least reliable and least valid test of ability in English composition. But if it did so, did it not thereby foster doubts about the validity of its own yardstick, the teachers' ratings of their students? Were not these ratings based on essays?

One enthusiastic test expert at the Educational Testing Service, discussing the experiment in a lecture, began by pointing out that the teachers, in addition to being highly capable, had known the students for at least a year, during which time each student had written over a dozen essays. This does seem to put the matter of the yardstick in a different light. But later in his lecture he decided to face the contention of teachers who give essay examinations that the grades they give on their finals agree remarkably well with the estimates of the abilities of their students that they have formed during the year. He explained this by referring to the halo effect, pointing out that teachers usually make up their minds about the abilities of their students by the end of the first couple of months, and that the subsequent grades they give are so greatly influenced by these early opinions that they merely confirm what he called the *mistakes* the teachers made initially.

Perhaps we should make allowances for his having been carried away by his enthusiasm—and by his own peculiar halo effect with regard to essay grades—but he does seem to contradict himself, first praising the fundamental standard, the teachers' ratings, because they were based on many essays spread over a year or more, and then explaining that, because of the halo effect, such judgments are apt to be mistaken and thus very much less valid than he had previously made them sound.

The College Entrance Examination Board occupies a key position in American education. What it does can not fail to affect what goes on in the schools. For example, Miss Jane Sehmann, Director of Admissions at Smith College, said early in 1961, "As a result of parental and other pressure, schools are substituting vocabulary drills and word study for meaningful work in reading and writing."

And, on this same topic, here are excerpts from a review by Dr. Louis C. Zahner, Head of the English Department at Groton School, of an essay test made by the Educational Testing Service (the review appears on page 358 of the *Fifth Mental Measurements Yearbook*): "Few teachers, administrators, or businessmen who employ the product of schools and colleges would deny that written composition is deteriorating. The wholesale substitution of objective tests for essay examinations in all subjects may well be a major cause of the deterioration; for testing influences teaching to a degree little short of control. . . . [This essay] test has the same sort of solid validity as that of a swimming test that requires the testee to swim in the water; it is not concerned about how the details of his anatomy as measured on land correlate with those of other swimmers of known ability."

How could the College Board allow itself to become so fascinated by the statistical magic of the test-makers as to forget its larger responsibility? In examining for general college admissions, it gave up essay tests not once but twice. When it first gave up essay tests there was protest. When, after its experiment with the *General Composition Test,* it gave up essays once more, the clamor for essays was stilled only momentarily, if at all. For three years the Board withstood the pressure and refused to make a change. Then, in 1960, largely because of a massive attack organized by Eugene S. Wilson, Dean of Admissions at Amherst College, the Board yielded ground. It did not give up its non-essay *English Composition Test,* but it offered, in addition, an essay test—of sorts. It gave the essay test under examination conditions in the usual manner, but it did not grade it. Instead, it sent ungraded copies of candidates' essays to those colleges that insisted on having them.

Is there not just a hint of inconsistency here? In seeking earlier to justify its abandonment of essay tests, the Board had argued eloquently that maintaining reasonably consistent standards in essay grading was difficult even under the best conditions, with teams of trained, experienced graders brought together in close and continuing consultation on standards. Yet it is apparently content to let the new essays be graded haphazardly on what it must presumably regard as almost a hit-or-miss basis. To be sure, the Board does not refer to these essays as essays but gives them the official name of *Writing Samples.* But does this make the tests any the less essay tests? Can it be that the Board did not really feel as strongly about the difficulty of grading essays as it seemed to when arguing so eloquently for the abandonment of essay tests of English composition?

By yielding to pressure from within and without and agreeing to give these ungraded essay tests, the Board would seem to make the important concession that its non-essay *English Composition Test* and the verbal part of its multiple-choice *Scholastic Aptitude Test* leave something significant to be desired as tests in English composition: for, if it does not concede this, people may feel that in reintroducing essay tests but not grading them it was acting with tongue in cheek and merely pandering to what it presumably regards as professorial superstition. Yet if it does concede this, does not its former abandonment of the essay tests seem something less than proper?

Chapter 8

National Merit

THOSE WHO PRODUCE and administer tests have strong
interests in defending their effectiveness, and they often
cite statistics to show that the high scores of those who
did well on the tests were confirmed by their later performance. Consider, for example, the National Merit
Scholarship Corporation, which each year awards many
millions of dollars' worth of college scholarships all over
the nation and gives valuable testimonials in the form of
certificates of merit to many thousands of runners-up. In
its annual report for 1959, it speaks with pride of the
accomplishments of the National Merit Scholars in college.
Among other things, it says "about 82 per cent [of the
scholars] rank in the top quarter of their classes even
though many have selected colleges of very high academic
standing."

This is a curious boast. In 1959, out of 478,991 candidates for the Merit Scholarships, all but 10,334 were
eliminated from further consideration because of their
scores on a qualifying test, and ultimately a mere 920
received Merit Scholarships. In four years, out of 959,683
candidates only 3,465 were awarded scholarships. The
scholars are certainly a select group. Yet we gather from

the Corporation's statement that not all of this presumed elite went to colleges of very high academic standing and that, nevertheless, almost 20 per cent of them failed to rank even in the first quarter of their classes. Do these facts encourage faith in the screening process?

Again, the Corporation says in its report that "the national examinations have been praised as among the best available for determining aptitude and readiness to profit from a college education," and nowhere does it make any adverse remarks about these tests (except inadvertently, as in the above boast).

The Corporation cannot always have been satisfied with its qualifying test, for in 1958 it not only made an abrupt change in the nature of the test but took the contract away from the Educational Testing Service and gave it to Science Research Associates.

What of the new National Merit tests? There are two reviews of the April 1958 test in the *Fifth Mental Measurements Yearbook*. One of them is, on the whole, favorable, though it does not give the glowing impression that the Corporation's words might convey to the unwary reader. The reviewer characterizes the quality of the individual questions as "acceptable," and he is by no means convinced that the new type of test is an improvement over the old. Of course, it is natural for the Corporation to put its case in as favorable a light as possible. Foundations and industrial corporations have entrusted it with the distribution of enormous sums of money for scholarships and it has become, willingly or not, a by no means negligible force in the affairs of the nation. So it is understandable that the Corporation did not take public notice of the other critic, who complains that data supplied along with the test by Science Research Associates "exhibited characteristics suggestive of too much emphasis on salesmanship," and cites "as a wholesome contrast" the literature prepared by Educational Testing Service for their earlier form of the test.

The critic goes on to point out, among other things, that the test "was not suited to its task of identifying potential scholarship recipients" because it was not difficult enough for the superior candidates, and that "considerable psychometric naivete is exhibited in several sections of the Technical Manual," a charge he documents by pointing out significant flaws in the interpretation of statistics. He remarks briefly that "some of the [questions] are poorly written." He says that the parts of the test that deal with social studies and natural science "measure almost entirely reading ability and general verbal aptitude," and in this connection he points out that the statistics cited by Science Research Associates show scores on the social studies part to be about as good a measure of ability in natural science as they are of ability in social studies, and vice versa. He ends with the following words: "In conclusion, the [qualifying test] and the literature distributed about it did not seem to be a step forward. The reviewer is concerned that assessment psychology has been retarded and may have lost ground through the production and use of this test. He is amazed and disturbed that such inferior work can be conducted and tolerated on such a large scale. It is hoped that it will not be repeated." The people who take the tests, of course, know nothing of such criticisms and the tests go merrily on.

*   *   *

A word of explanation is in order before we proceed. The above, from the start of this chapter to the line of asterisks, is reproduced verbatim* from my article in the March, 1961, issue of *Harper's Magazine*. Naturally, the National Merit Scholarship Corporation did not remain

* Except that "latest annual report" has been changed to "annual report for 1959."

silent. J. M. Stalnaker, President of the Corporation, sent the editors the following letter, part of which was published in the May, 1961, issue of *Harper's*. Through the courtesy of Mr. Stalnaker, I am able to quote the original letter here in full:

We need more Banesh Hoffmanns to keep the test constructor alert and humble. But we also need to maintain our perspective and balance. "Beyond all reasonable doubts," said Carl Spearman, the late distinguished English scientist, "the tests do proffer such potent aid to life that their renunciation would be suicidal."

Even so, we all enjoy nit-picking at test items. Many test items should be improved and they will be. But the larger, more fundamental question is this: what method of measuring human intellectual attainment and promise, regardless of the time or money required, is superior to the tests about which Dr. Hoffmann complains?

As for his comments on the National Merit Scholarship Program, he is delightfully confused and misinformed. For instance, the preliminary screening test used in the Merit Program is completely revised and improved each year, as is the technical manual. Each test we have used, however, has been ideally suited in difficulty to the group tested, regardless of what one uninformed critic may have said.

In the Merit Program we use two tests, prepared by different testing agencies. But we also use students' school records, records of accomplishments outside the classroom, and the judgments of school officials. Finally, all of this information is evaluated not by a machine (although some persons believe it should be), but by experienced, skilled educators who make the actual selection of the National Merit Scholars.

As to the Merit Scholars themselves, and their degree of success, Dr. Hoffmann exhibits ignorance both of able youth and of the system of higher education in this country. He apparently believes that every Merit Scholar should conform at once by obtaining all A grades in the college of his choice and in the curriculum he has elected, both unwisely chosen in some cases.

We select Merit Scholars from every conceivable background—state, community, home, school—and offer them free choice of college and curriculum because we believe freedom of choice should be preserved. A very few are not prepared to fit immediately into the radically different intellectual and social environment they select. A few independent youngsters think that grades are relatively unimportant and pursue knowledge in their own creative way even at the expense of A grades.

Yet make no mistake about it, the academic performance of the total group of Merit Scholars is amazing. What other selection techniques have done as effective a job?

The Merit Program's important research activities are uncovering ways in which we can improve the selection methods. We are experimenting, for example, with practical ways to find the more creative, highly motivated students.

During the past five years, the Merit Program has contributed significantly to producing greater public recognition, respect, and honor for intellectual endeavors. It has motivated many students to pursue more diligently their own intellectual development. It has helped thousands of able students to obtain scholarship help from a great variety of sources.

These are vital national objectives. If others can devise more effective ways to reach them, we shall be among the first to adopt the new procedures. Dr. Hoffmann might well ponder the classic remark of Bruce Bairnsfather's Old Bill to his complaining companion in a shell hole: "If you can find a better 'ole, 'op to it."

This is a cleverly reassuring letter. Few who read it hastily will appreciate its subtlety.

In 1959, the National Merit Scholarship Corporation eliminated some 98 per cent of the candidates from further consideration because of their scores on a multiple-choice qualifying test, and subsequently eliminated about one tenth of one per cent more because of their scores on the *Scholastic Aptitude Test* of the College Board. Since these 1959 percentages are typical, we see that a mere 2 per cent of the candidates are given detailed consideration. The situation is even worse than this, since the scholarships are awarded state by state rather than on a nationwide basis, the result being that in some states only those students are given detailed consideration whose multiple-choice test scores fall well within the top one per cent according to the national scale, the rest being summarily rejected. But note how soothingly Mr. Stalnaker handles this crucial point. The only relevant passage in his letter is this:

In the Merit Program we use two tests, prepared by different testing agencies. But we also use students' school records, records of accomplishment outside the classroom, and the judgments of school officials. Finally, all of this information is evaluated not by a machine (although some persons believe it should be), but by experienced, skilled educators who make the actual selection of the National Merit Scholars.

What Mr. Stalnaker says here is true, of course. But will the hasty reader be likely to realize that his remarks apply to only 2 per cent of the candidates? And that the matter of the summary elimination of 98 per cent of the candidates by means of multiple-choice tests has not been touched upon at all?

Mr. Stalnaker has an ambivalent attitude towards college grades. They are indeed, as he suggests, unreliable as measures of ability and achievement. Yet, with all their faults, they are the principal standard against which statistical testers measure the validity of scholastic aptitude tests. To point up the deficiencies of college grades, as Mr. Stalnaker now does, is thus to cast doubt on the value of scholastic aptitude tests—an activity I have no desire to hinder. But the Corporation itself used class rank in college as its standard when it made its boast in the 1959 report, and nowhere in that report did it hint at the frailty of the standard. Is a critic now to be scolded for using the Corporation's own standard in scrutinizing its boast?

Again, Mr. Stalnaker gives the reader the impression that all is well with the tests, and implies that a single adverse review need not be taken seriously. How can one counter such bland reassurances when the tests are relatively secret and only the April, 1958, tests were available for review in the *Fifth Mental Measurements Yearbook*? Of the two reviews there, one was absolutely scathing and the other by no means enthusiastic. The former was written by Professor Benno G. Fricke, Assistant Chief of the Evaluations and Examinations Division at the University of Michigan—a man whom Mr. Stalnaker dismisses as "one uninformed critic."

Perhaps the following will indicate further that the 1958 tests left something to be desired. In the *Fifth Mental Measurements Yearbook* there are two reviews of the *Scholarship Qualifying Tests* made by the Educational Testing Service, these being the tests that the National Merit Scholarship Corporation gave up in favor of the new tests made by Science Research Associates.

One of these two reviewers is Professor Lee J. Cronbach of the University of Illinois, author of one of the best-regarded books on testing. After saying, in favor of the test, that "the best 'cramming' [for the test] would be that sort of training in reading and reasoning which will also make [the student] a better college prospect," Professor Cronbach adds this gratuitous parenthetical remark: "(In this respect, the test by another publisher which replaced the SQT in the 1958 National Merit Scholarship testing is inferior. Some items in the new test call for knowledge of crammable grammatical rules, and the use of uncommon words in its verbal section makes almost reasonable the conduct of the reviewer's young acquaintance who prepared for the competition by reading through a dictionary.)"

What is significant about this quotation is not only what is said but, even more, the fact that, in such a place, it was said at all, for gratuitous parenthetical remarks of this sort are not apt to be made without the prompting of strong feeling. (I add at this point my own gratuitous parenthetical remark. The reviewer quoted above, speaking now of the test he is actually reviewing, says: "The test is designed for steady pacers. The intuitive, nonconformist hare, darting here and there after brilliant ideas, will be left behind," a crucial and widely applicable criticism whose impact is by no means softened by his continuing with the words "but so will the drudging tortoises of academic life.")

Many of the National Merit Scholars are extremely able. Yet, if multiple-choice tests tend even only slightly to penalize the deep, subtle, creative students and favor those who are quick-witted and superficially brilliant, their use as the *sole* non-geographical criterion for the automatic rejection of 98 per cent of the candidates for National Merit Scholarships is indefensible, except on the grounds of sheer expediency. When only 2 per cent of the candidates pass, and the competition is keen, it does not take more than a few subtly defective questions to play havoc with the chances of the deep, probing candidates. Some testers defend the use of College Board tests in connection with college admissions on the ground that the test scores are used in conjunction with other data, and that only those students who score quite poorly on these tests are likely to be automatically denied full consideration by competent admissions officers. But such a defence, by conceding the fallibility of the tests, points up the weakness of the National Merit procedure. One sympathizes with the Corporation, confronted as it is by a staggering task. Yet considering that the candidates are far from being run-of-the-mill students, and that the scholarships are intended for some of the very best students in the country, one must deplore the Corporation's heavy reliance on multiple-choice tests. To select National Merit Scholars from among only those who survive the elimination test and the subsequent *Scholastic Aptitude Test* is to do a disservice to education by exaggerating and glorifying the merits of such tests.

Does the Corporation hold the tests in high esteem? Does it believe they are essentially free of important inadequacies? One might think so from Mr. Stalnaker's letter, especially when one finds him asking rhetorically "what method of measuring human intellectual attainment and promise, *regardless of the time or money required,* is superior to the tests about which Dr. Hoffmann complains?" But in fact the Corporation is well aware of at least some of these inadequacies, and is aware of them not on the basis of subjective opinion, which some statistical testers tend to scorn, but on such testers' own favored basis of statistics. There is a hint of this in Mr. Stalnaker's letter, where, having allowed a decent interval to elapse after the rhetorical query just quoted, he says, "We are experimenting, for example, with practical ways to find the more creative, highly motivated students." There is, of course, no contradiction between these two quoted passages if one is ready to agree that "intellectual attainment and promise" do not significantly involve creativity and a high degree of motivation. But let us not allow ourselves to be sidetracked by a matter of subjective opinion. We are concerned here with the extent of the Corporation's realization of these significant inadequacies of multiple-choice tests.

The Corporation makes extensive and important research studies of a statistical nature—though, unfortunately, it does not appear to have made the crucial study of comparing the performance of those candidates who scored, in each state, in the top 2 per cent, with those who scored in the 96 per cent to 98 per cent group, those in the 94 per cent to 96 per cent group, and so on. In one of its statistical investigations, Dr. John L. Holland, who is the Director of Research of the National Merit Scholarship Corporation, studied almost one thousand of the 2 per cent of the candidates who were not summarily eliminated because of their scores on the 1959 tests. His results were reported in an article, "Creative and Academic Performance among Talented Adolescents," which appeared in the *Journal of Educational Psychology* in 1961. Among other things, he and his assistants calculated over ten thousand correlations, into whose nature we need not enter. What interests us here is the following conclusion drawn by Dr. Holland from his statistical study, a conclusion the gist of which is accurately presented in the Corporation's 1960 report. Admittedly, the study was concerned with only the 2 per cent who passed the qualifying multiple-choice test, but it would be remarkable if the conclusion were to prove applicable solely to this sort of group. Here is what Dr. Holland said:

Perhaps the most unequivocal finding in the present study is that, for samples of students of superior scholastic aptitude [meaning of students who were not among the 98 per cent summarily rejected], creative performance is generally unrelated to scholastic achievement and scholastic aptitude. Since the traditional predictors of scholastic aptitude are of little or no value for predicting creativity, it seems clear that scholarship programs, colleges, and other agencies, if they are concerned primarily with rewarding students or selecting employees who have potential for creative performance, need to make a more active effort to devise predictors of creative potential. In fact, attempts to build better scholastic aptitude tests may even be detrimental, since they may lead to a greater dependence on instruments which are of limited value and thus delay unnecessarily the development of efficient predictors of creative performance.

Chapter 9

Statistics

MANY INTELLIGENT PEOPLE have expressed concern about the defects of multiple-choice tests. But when the more experienced testers are faced with general criticisms they are inclined to smile indulgently. In their view, criticisms unbacked by specific statistics may be dismissed as mere opinion.

Yet such criticisms, coming from responsible people, should not be lightly brushed aside as the opinions of outsiders or as idle thoughts lacking a basis of statistical evidence. Statistics are no substitute for intellectual standards, nor are they a shield against all types of criticism. Their use by people who.lack insight can have disastrous consequences.

Even in uncomplicated situations the significance of statistics is not always clear. Are statistics likely to be unequivocal, then, in so delicate and complex an activity as the assessment of human beings? Since the testers build their tests on a statistical foundation, and defend their tests statistically, it will be well to look briefly into the matter of statistics. At the least, this will help executives, teachers, and members of PTA's to resist the statistical blandishments of the testers and their supporters.

For all the tester's deriding of judgment, he can not escape dependence on it. In the last analysis, no proper merit rating can be made without appeal to judgment. If, by an elaborate statistical routine, the tester constructs, for example, a test of scholastic aptitude, he can not know whether his test is valid until he compares its predictions, directly or indirectly, with such things as actual college grades. These grades are given by professors, not by machines. They are the result of professorial judgment —except when the professors themselves rely wholly on multiple-choice tests, and even then they go back to other professors' judgments. If a statistical tester justifies his use of "objective," statistical procedures by first deriding judgment, he weakens his claims that his tests do indeed measure what they are said to measure when he validates the test against judgments, as, basically, he must. Yet if he does not deride judgment he weakens his initial case for the use of his "objective" tests.

He will, on occasion, argue that freshman grades, for example, are the result of judgments made by many professors in many subjects, in many institutions, and that, although individually the standards of the professors, the degrees of difficulty of the subjects, and the academic aspirations of the colleges undoubtedly vary widely, statistically these discrepancies tend to cancel out. If pressed, he will ask, in somewhat bewildered tones, what other possible standard of scholastic aptitude there could be. By so doing, he betrays his bias towards the numerical. Why should there be a standard of "scholastic aptitude" when, for all we know, there is no such specific thing as "scholastic aptitude" in the first place? Is it not a numerical invention? If by "scholastic aptitude" we mean some combination of relatively superficial, numerically measurable, verbal and arithmetical traits that are correlated with professorial grades with all their crotchets, idiosyncrasies, and exceptions, are we not talking of a smoothed-out, carefully sandpapered, statistical monstrosity that is barely better than iquination?

Sometimes the standard the tester uses is the test itself. For example, when the tester wants to try out questions for a later version of a test that already exists, he may include these new questions, on an experimental basis, as extra questions on the existing test, heedless of the psychological effect the presence of these unscreened questions will have on the superior students—the very ones who are able to perceive their faults. The tester will gather statistics concerning the experimental questions, noting how effective each was in discriminating between the "best" students and the others so that he can determine objectively which questions to include on the new version of the test. To discover which students are the "best," what could be more convenient for the tester than to use the scores on the regular part of the test? After all, the test has already been validated. Not to use it as a standard would be tantamount to an admission of doubt as to its validity. The procedure seems reasonable. But this incestuous mating of statistics with their kin serves to perpetuate faults as well as virtues. Its main effect is to homogenize. It makes each succeeding version of the test essentially a replica of the original, even if the new version has different questions, and even different *types* of questions.

If the original test favored the quick-reading, superficially brilliant, cynically test-wise candidate, and penalized the intellectually honest candidate with a subtle, probing, critical, or creative mind, then subsequent versions will do just the same. The inbred statistics gathered by the testmaker will reflect the homogenization that his procedure has imposed, but they will not reveal that what was homogenized and perpetuated was something warped. These inbred statistics will show gratifying consistency between the old and the new versions of the test, but they will not reveal the grave imperfections of the test as an instrument for selecting the best candidates, in any sense of the word "best" other than that so one-sidedly defined by the test itself. On the contrary, the deceptive consistency of these, as of other, incestuous statistics produces a false sense of security, contentment, and scientific justification, and becomes a convenient device for stifling criticism and convincing the unwary.

Not all of the statistics used by the testers are inbred, of course. But those that are not inbred are apt to have a far less impressive air. In Chapter 7 we quoted Professor Carroll on the matter of reading readiness tests; referring to the ability of a "pretty good" reading readiness test to predict reading success at the end of the first year, he spoke of correlations of about .60 as being "quite good." Since the *Scholastic Aptitude Tests* of the College Entrance Examination Board have a correlation with freshman grades in college of about .50 we are tempted to conclude that these tests are not quite "quite good." But how good is this "quite good"?

Correlations measure how much relationship there is between one set of data and another. Their values run from −1 to 1, with 0 corresponding to complete lack of linear relationship between the two sets of data, and both −1 and 1 corresponding to rigorous relationship admitting no exceptions at all. The negative correlations occur when one score tends to rise as the comparison score falls, as occurs, for example, when one compares the number of polio shots given in a community with the number of subsequent cases of polio.

Suppose we found ourselves under orders to report the heights of several thousand adult men, but were not allowed to see the men. And suppose that all we were allowed to know about them was their names, their weights, and their IQ's. If we relied solely on their IQ's and the lengths of their names, our report would almost certainly have a correlation of zero, or thereabouts, with the actual heights. Clearly we would have to rely on the men's weights. We might, for example, assign to each man the average height of men of his approximate weight. But we would have little confidence in the accuracy of our report. Thin men would obviously be rated far too short and fat men far too tall.

Suppose now that we were allowed to compare our report, based as it was on the men's weights, with the men's actual heights and calculate the correlation we had achieved. We would feel some trepidation about the outcome, and rightly so. But, assuming that we had been neither particularly lucky nor particularly unlucky, we would find that, according to this statistical criterion, we had actually performed our task somewhat better than the College Board predicts college freshman grades by means of its *Scholastic Aptitude Tests,* though somewhat worse than the reading readiness testers cited by Professor Carroll predicted reading success.

Though there is greater objectivity in heights than in college grades, the above indicates a degree of fallibility in even "quite good" tests that should give us pause.

A correlation of .50 is not five-sixths as good as one of .60. Correlations are not so simple as that, by any means. Suppose we wish to predict the grades that a group of students will get in college and, lacking any relevant information, we guess their grades at random, or we assign the grades alphabetically, or we "predict" that every student will receive the average grade. Such predictions will be worthless, of course, and, under normal circumstances, each would have a correlation of zero or thereabouts with the actual grades. Suppose, now, that we make a new prediction based on scores on an appropriate test made by a responsible and respected test-maker. Under normal circumstances the new prediction will be better than any of the old ones—even the bitterest critics of tests would concede that! But how much better? If we made a perfect prediction the correlation would be unity. But we are unlikely to have been as lucky as that. Suppose we achieved a correlation of .60. We could find from it the amount by which we had sharpened the precision of our worthless "predictions" by calculating what is called the percentage of *forecasting efficiency*. This statistical quantity tells us the extent to which we have succeeded in narrowing what we may loosely refer to here as the statistical size of our error, and it is a not unreasonable measure of our success. As we would expect, our original "predictions" would turn out to have a forecasting efficiency of 0 per cent or thereabouts, and our perfect prediction one of 100 per cent. But our test with a correlation of .60 would have a forecasting efficiency of only 20 per cent. A correlation of .50 corresponds to a 13 per cent improvement. Even a correlation of .70 yields only a 29 per cent improvement, as here measured, and it is a rare test indeed that has as high a validity correlation as this.

Whichever way we prefer to look at correlations, college entrance tests that barely achieve a correlation of .50 with college freshman grades can hardly be regarded as wholly trustworthy guides. Many colleges, of course, realizing this, do not take the *Scholastic Aptitude Test* scores very seriously. Unfortunately, other colleges do, even though the College Board itself repeatedly urges them not to place too great reliance on these scores and certainly not to use them as the sole, or even the principal criterion for deciding who shall be excluded from college. For example, in an address, "Candidates and Confusion," published in the Summer, 1957, issue of *College and University,* Dr. Frank H. Bowles, newly-elected president of the College Board, said: "The use of tests to support arbitrary admissions restrictions is deplorable. Tests are only substitutes for judgment, not judgment, and counsellors and admissions officers must curb their instinct to accept this substitute when time presses."

Statistics, for all their scientific aura, can be highly misleading. As a fanciful illustration, we can imagine statisticians of an earlier generation discovering a remarkably high correlation between supreme musical virtuosity and length of hair—at least, in the case of males. Yet this would hardly have justified their using length of hair in place of the subjective judgment of musicians as a measure of musical virtuosity on the grounds that it was objective and the correlation was excellent.

Even when statistics are undeniably relevant they pertain to the masses and not to the individual, and this has serious implications that go beyond the obvious occurrence of exceptions and injustices. For whatever is exceptional is, by its very nature, rare; and being rare, it makes no statistical splash. Normalcy and mediocrity are common, and statistics tend to be dominated by what is average. Being based on the past, and reflecting mistrust of individual judgment, they favor conformity, and, in general, penalize innovation. The people rated highest according to statistically-based norms are apt to be the brilliant representatives of mediocrity at its pinnacle. This would not be undesirable if high ability of an unusual type were comparably rewarded. But abilities, such as profundity and originality, that differ in kind from those possessed by the mediocre are not an intensification of something widely possessed, and because of their rarity they do not significantly shape the statistical norm.

Related to this are two basic flaws in the correlations used by the multiple-choice testers: the facts that these correlations treat all people as equally important, and that they do not distinguish between bias and mere random error.

For example, suppose that a hundred candidates take

a multiple-choice test in science, and that an Einstein among them, probing too deeply, comes out tenth instead of first. Under normal circumstances, the effect on the validity correlation will be just the same as that of an utter moron, fortunate in his guessing, coming out tenth from the last instead of last.

Let us go further. Suppose that the hundred candidates were competing for nine scholarships, and that while the Einstein still came out tenth from the top, the moron came out twentieth from the bottom. The moron's misplacement would now have a greater impact on the correlation than would the misplacement of the Einstein. The Einstein would be denied a scholarship; but the statistical correlation would rate this as a lesser calamity than the misplacement of the moron, though the latter misplacement had no effect at all on the selection of scholarship winners.

Let us go further still. Suppose we wish to eliminate all but 2 per cent of scholarship candidates on the basis of test scores alone. If we had a test having a correlation of .90 with subsequent performance—there is no such miraculous test, of course—we would be likely to feel enormous confidence in its validity. But now let us imagine we have two such tests, each with a correlation of .90: one of the tests has a slight bias against the supremely gifted candidates, rating them 3 per cent or 4 per cent from the top instead of in the top 2 per cent; the other has a slight bias in favor of the most moronic candidates, rating them 3 per cent or 4 per cent from the bottom instead of in the lowest 2 per cent.

For ordinary guidance purposes the two tests would be of equal merit, and extraordinarily high merit it might well be. But as instruments for the elimination of 98 per cent of the candidates, the merits of the second test, with its slight bias in favor of morons, would far transcend those of the first, with its slight bias against the best candidates.

Indeed, a test that gave correct ratings to the top 2 per cent but appallingly erroneous ratings to the other 98 per cent might have an over-all correlation of .10 or worse; and yet it would have perfect validity for our particular purpose. For if only 2 per cent of the candidates pass, it makes no difference where a failing candidate is placed among the 98 per cent that fail, even though the 98 per cent have by far the greater effect on the usual correlations.

People who put their trust in correlations would do well to heed Aesop's fable, "The Lioness and the Fox": "A lioness who was being belittled by a fox for always bearing just one cub said, 'Yes, but it's a lion.' "*

A person who uses statistics does not thereby automatically become a scientist, any more than a person who uses a stethoscope automatically becomes a doctor. Nor is an activity necessarily scientific just because statistics are used in it.

The most important thing to understand about reliance on statistics in a field such as testing is that such reliance warps perspective. The person who holds that subjective judgment and opinion are suspect and decides that only statistics can provide the objectivity and relative certainty that he seeks, begins by unconsciously ignoring, and ends by consciously deriding, whatever can not be given a numerical measure or label. His sense of values becomes distorted. He comes to believe that whatever is non-numerical is inconsequential. He can not serve two masters. If he worships statistics he will simplify, fractionalize, distort, and cheapen in order to force things into a numerical mold.

The multiple-choice tester who meets criticisms by merely citing test statistics shows either his contempt for the intelligence of his readers or else his personal lack of

* Quoted with permission from *Aesop Without Morals,* translated and edited by Lloyd W. Daly (New York: Thomas Yoseloff, 1961).

concern for the non-numerical aspects of testing, importantly among them the deleterious effects his test procedures have on education. His statistical justifications give no weight to dangerous side effects, side effects that, for example, prompted the New York State Teachers Association to pass a resolution in 1961 urging the New York State Board of Regents to concentrate on improving essay questions for examinations instead of attempting to develop completely objective tests. He is a little like a television executive who evaluates programs solely on the basis of the amounts of money they make—on the ground that numerical data of this sort are scientific and precise, while matters of conscience, propriety, responsibility, and good taste, being non-numerical, may be safely and properly ignored. We would not be overly surprised to hear him advocate replacing the Supreme Court by a computer.

Because the statistics usually cited as justification for the use of multiple-choice tests ignore the non-numerical aspects of both testing and its side effects, they are, in fact, far from being accurate measures of the whole merit or lack of merit of current test procedures.

The purpose of this chapter is mainly to undermine excessive faith in statistics—a fact that may not have escaped the attention of the reader. But since the testers cite statistical evidence in support of their tests and tend to scoff at non-statistical criticisms, it is not inappropriate to show that the testers are vulnerable even on their own statistical ground.

If a parent were to ask a school principal why so much emphasis is placed on IQ's in the selection of students for special placement, he would probably be told that correlations with school and college grades show that IQ's are a good indication of scholastic aptitude. Neither he nor the principal would be likely to know that these correlations would not reveal biases that IQ tests may have against particular types of gifted students.

Recently, however, psychologists have been exploring the possibility of measuring creativity objectively. In attempting to assess this attribute numerically, they naturally abandon the multiple-choice, pick-the-one-"best"-answer concept. They give candidates tasks that are deliberately chosen to allow considerable freedom of response. For example, they may give the candidate an unfinished "drawing" consisting of a few meaningless lines and ask him to complete the picture in as many novel ways as he can. The candidates are rated not on how closely their responses resemble a single "best" answer. On the contrary, they are rated, roughly speaking, on the number of responses they can produce that are significantly *different* from those produced by the majority, this grading criterion being, of course, explained to them before they start the test.

There are many variations of both test tasks and scoring methods that we have not gone into here. And there are various questions that one might wish to raise about the whole procedure. But it is clear that these tests are, in a crucial sense, just the opposite of multiple-choice tests.

Professors J. W. Getzels and P. W. Jackson, of the University of Chicago, made an experiment using tests of the new type. At a secondary school with 449 students, they selected two contrasted groups: in the one that they called the "high creativity group" they listed students who scored in the top 20 per cent on the new tests but were not in the top 20 per cent according to their IQ scores; in the one that they called the "high intelligence group" they listed students who were in the top 20 per cent on the basis of their IQ's but not in the top 20 per cent according to the new tests. There was a sizable difference in the average IQ's, on the Binet scale, of the two groups: that of the "high creativity group" was 127, which was actually lower than the average IQ, 132, of the whole school, while that of the "high intelligence group" was

150. One should not imagine that an IQ of 150 is only slightly higher than one of 127. Some 8.2 per cent of Americans have Binet IQ's in the range 120 to 129, 3.1 per cent in the range 130 to 139, 1.1 per cent in the range 140 to 149, and a mere 0.2 per cent in the range 150 to 159. Roughly speaking, this means that while one person in about 20 scores 127 or higher, only one in 500 scores 150 or higher.

The "school performance" of each of the two groups above was assessed by computing average scores on standardized achievement tests of the usual multiple-choice type—tests that, by their nature, would tend to favor the "high intelligence group," which had been selected because of its high scores on tests of a basically similar type.

What was the result? Despite their different average IQ's, the two groups turned out to have essentially the same "school performance" averages. Specifically, the "high intelligence group" had an average of 55, and the "high creativity group" an average of 56—this despite the fact that the multiple-choice scholastic achievement tests gave the "creative" students no chance to exhibit their superior "creativity." Professor E. P. Torrance, of the University of Minnesota, conducted more extensive studies along the same lines. His results, on the whole, though not in every instance, were in basic accord with those of Getzels and Jackson.

In view of the above, how much faith can we have in the IQ as an unbiased predictor of scholastic achievement, even when the scholastic achievement is measured by multiple-choice methods? Think of the number of gifted students who are penalized in our schools because they lack the IQ knack.

We conclude this chapter by telling of a large-scale statistical study of the effectiveness of tests made by Professors Robert L. Thorndike and Elizabeth Hagen, both of Teachers College, Columbia University. It is reported in their book *Ten Thousand Careers,* published by Wiley in 1959.

During World War II, the United States Army Air Force brought together a staff of professional psychologists to develop a battery of tests to differentiate between potential pilots, navigators, and bombardiers. The tests were administered to over half a million men, but Professors Thorndike and Hagen confined their study to 17,000 men who had been given one particular version of the test battery in the latter half of 1943. The authors succeeded in obtaining follow-up information from somewhat more than 10,000 of these men in 1955 and 1956.

The Army Air Force tests had been elaborate, the battery consisting of some twenty different parts, among which, in addition to a lengthy biographical questionnaire, were tests of such things as reading comprehension, general information, arithmetic reasoning, mathematics, the reading of instrument dials, speed of identification, complex co-ordination, and finger dexterity.

From the information they obtained in 1955 and 1956, the authors sorted the men into 124 different categories according to their current occupations, and then estimated how successful they were in their occupations, using for this purpose seven different criteria, such as income earned, number of men supervised, feeling of success, and length of time in the occupation. With the indispensable aid of electronic computers, they then calculated, among other things, the correlations between each test and each criterion of success for each of 90 occupations—some 12,000 correlations in all.

What did they discover as a result of this massive undertaking? Among other things, that from a man's answers on the biographical questionnaire questions about his education, such as whether he had spent any time in college before entering the Army Air Force, or how he had made out in physics or trigonometry, one could infer, though with limited success, the general sort of occupation he would find himself in later on; that such a question as how often he had performed the job of adjusting a carburetor also had predictive value as to the nature of his job; and that the scores on the aptitude tests had comparably limited predictive value.

So far, so good, if hardly unexpected or exciting. But what of the question of success and satisfaction in an occupation once a man was in it? Here is the carefully worded verdict of the investigators on this crucial matter:

As far as we were able to determine from our data, there is no convincing evidence that aptitude tests or biographical information of the type that was available to us can predict degree of success within an occupation insofar as this is represented in the criterion measures that we were able to obtain. This would suggest that we should view the long-range prediction of occupational success by aptitude tests with a good deal of skepticism and take a very restrained view as to how much can be accomplished in this direction.

Chapter 10

Challenge to the Testers

UNDERMINING BLIND FAITH in statistics is crucially important. But it does not exorcise statistics—nor is it meant to. For statistics, when viewed with healthy skepticism, can be a valuable and often indispensable tool.

Unfortunately, even when the layman is amply forewarned he is apt to be helpless against experts who wish to influence him by statistical arguments. Undermining blind faith in statistics, therefore, has only limited effect. It may weaken the impact of statistical arguments, but that alone is not enough to bring about reforms in testing.

Nor are general criticisms of multiple-choice testing effective in bringing about reforms, as has been abundantly demonstrated. It is not difficult to find prominent educators and other commentators who have launched wide-ranging general protests against the tests. William H. Whyte, Jr., in *The Organization Man* (Simon and Schuster, 1956; Doubleday Anchor Books, 1957), and Professor Jacques Barzun, in *The House of Intellect* (Harper, 1959; Harper Torchbooks, 1962), are but two of the more recent. These writers and others have made many charges against the tests. The indictment is long. For example:

The tests deny the creative person a significant opportunity to demonstrate his creativity, and favor the shrewd and facile candidate over the one who has something of his own to say. Unlike essay examinations, they are mainly concerned with predetermined intellectual snippets, and not with the crucial ability to conceive, design, and actually carry out a complex undertaking in an individual way.

They penalize the candidate who perceives subtle points unnoticed by less able people, including the test-makers. They are apt to be superficial and intellectually dishonest, with questions made artificially difficult by means of ambiguity because genuinely searching questions do not readily fit into the multiple-choice format.

They take account only of the choice of answer and not of the quality of thought that led to the choice.

They too often degenerate into subjective guessing games in which the candidate does not pick what he considers the best answer out of a bad lot but rather the one he believes the unknown examiner would consider the best.

They neglect skill in disciplined expression.

They have a pernicious effect on education and the recognition of merit.

One might think that criticisms such as these would have significant repercussions. But they are *general* criticisms and as such do not seem to disturb the multiple-choice testers.

Some critics of multiple-choice tests have spoken gently. For example, Dr. Benjamin F. Wright, when president of Smith College, wrote in his annual report for 1955–56:

. . . the examinations given by the College Board authorities consist of objective questions. There are no essay or discussion type questions, and the answers can be graded mechanically. Such examinations are less than perfect when it comes to indicating how effectively the student can make use of information, or even the quality of understanding of subject matter. They seem, moreover, to give the advantage to certain kinds of minds, although not always to those which will take the greatest advantage of college opportunities.

Others have spoken more sharply. For example, Dr. R. C. Derbyshire, a member of the Executive Committee of the Federation of State Medical Boards, wrote in the December, 1961, issue of the journal RISS*:

. . . It's time someone disputed the infallibility of the psychologists and pointed out the glaring fallacies of the so-called objective examinations.

Unlike psychology, medicine still does not claim to be an exact science. The studious and thoughtful candidate taking a multiple-choice examination would carefully consider various possibilities and often conclude rightly that more than one answer could be correct.

And a professor of physics at one of our most distinguished universities, who wishes to remain anonymous, wrote to me in April, 1961, as follows:

I personally consider [multiple-choice tests] the greatest menace in the whole U. S. educational system. . . . aside from not accomplishing their avowed purpose of testing they completely ignore the other and equally important role of examinations—their effect on teaching and learning.

As to the quality of tests in general, here is an excerpt from pages 323 and 324 of the book *Measurement for Guidance,* by Professors John W. M. Rothney, Paul J. Danielson, and Robert A. Heimann (Harper, 1959):

One possible way to improve tests would be to declare a moratorium on the production of new testing instruments for a period of years. During the period obsolete and poorly conceived tests would be killed off, gains would be consolidated, and standards of test design and marketing might be

* National Magazine for Residents, Internes, and Senior Students.

strengthened. Unfortunately, such a plan can hardly be taken seriously, for the attractiveness of profits from test production and marketing is too great for many persons to resist. It does seem strange, however, in a country in which butchers' and grocers' scales are regularly checked and policed, and clothiers' tags of "100 percent wool" must be validated if the sellers of such products are to avoid imprisonment, that a test distributor may sell his products without any supervision or regulation. After reading many test manuals one is often left with the feeling that "there ought to be a law." And it may come to that. It seems to have been assumed in the past that educational or psychological tests could be produced and distributed without any kind of regulation. It has been found necessary to enforce compliance with Pure Food and Drug Acts to protect even professional persons, who, presumably, should not need protection. Perhaps educators, psychologists, and counselors need similar legislation for protection from those who have taken advantage of freedom from control.

Students are well aware of the shortcomings of multiple-choice tests. Here, for example, are excerpts from a letter sent to me by Linden M. Lovegren, a National Merit Scholar:

I once had a teacher justify his choice of an answer [on a classroom multiple-choice test] by saying "I like that one the best, although they're all right answers," or, "None of them are any good, but this one comes the closest to being possible." Also, the tests most teachers devise put a premium on remembering individual bits and pieces of information, and the better grades go to those with better memories. . . .

I will say that the tests measure one ability—the ability to learn how to take the tests. This ability does not correlate well with school grades. . . . And I'm also sure that many people who placed below me on the CEEB and NMSC tests turn in better classroom performances than I, and not because I'm not trying!

In short, one of the best pieces of advice to give on "how

to take multiple-choice tests" is this: Play your hunches. If you stop to think, you'll only get confused.

There is no need here to discuss in detail the activities of the professional testers in the world of business. They were dealt with deftly and devastatingly by William H. Whyte, Jr., in his book *The Organization Man.* When an intelligent layman sees actual "tests" of personality traits and the like he is apt to think them not just absurd but, in view of the uses to which they are put, menacingly so. But because seemingly hardheaded business executives appear to place great confidence in these "tests," we present two quotations concerning their merits.

The first is taken from the *Guide to Evaluation of Employees for Promotion,* put out by the United States Civil Service Commission in March, 1959, "as a working tool and resource for [governmental] agencies in developing and improving their plans under the Merit Promotion Program." Here are excerpts from pages 20 and 25:

It is very doubtful that [questionnaires designed to identify interest patterns and personality or temperament traits], at their present stage of development, have practical value generally in selection of personnel . . . inventory forms which are readily susceptible to distortion by the applicant and difficult to "score" are not likely to contribute to sound personnel decisions, except where individual counseling and placement is a major feature of the program. . . .

Certainly, personal characteristics are significant to job success. However, the use of personality tests to evaluate these should be approached with great care. Many people know what behaviors or attitudes are approved or expected, and on a test can readily indicate the "correct" answers even when, in fact, their attitudes and behavior are much different.

Defenders of these personality "tests" may try to counter this by pointing to the presence, in certain of these "tests," of special trap questions intended to catch the candidates who are lying. But would they have us believe that the United States Civil Service Commission was unaware of the presence of these traps?

The second quotation is taken from pages 283 and 284 of the book *Measurement for Guidance,* by Rothney, Danielson, and Heimann, which we have already cited. It discusses the use of these "tests" by guidance counselors:

There is a great deal of evidence that personality questionnaires, controlled interviews, and interest inventories are widely used in counseling. Just why this should be so in view of the demonstrated inadequacies of these devices is difficult to understand. It seems that it must be a combination of amazing, psychometric innocence on the part of the users, naivete in considering the counseling job as a "quickie" affair rather than a complex longitudinal problem, mistaken faith in statistics on the part of inventory producers and consumers, expediency, and a desire to keep up with the other fellow who uses them for any of the above reasons. Perhaps another reason for their popularity can be found in the seeming exactness they give to the counselor's work. Counseling interviews may seem not scientifically respectable enough to impress one's colleagues or clients, but an array of scores might possibly do so. The popularity of the instruments may be due in part, then, to the psychological support that counselors, working in a relatively new area, and without adequate evidence of their effectiveness, may feel that they need; and the round-the-clock hucksterism in the sales of the instruments must account in large measure for their widespread use. Certainly it cannot be justified on the basis of logical reasoning or experimental evidence.

Clearly there is reason enough to believe that all is not well in the field of testing. But the test-makers are well entrenched and grow more powerful every day. They know that their clients find it difficult to withstand their blandishments, for they offer a service that has almost irresistible attractions: they undertake to supply neatly packaged numerical valuations of personnel, quickly and objectively, with scientific precision and a minimum of inconvenience —and all for a relatively modest fee.

The test-makers have developed a strikingly effective routine for dealing with their critics. When confronted with general criticisms that they find they can not simply ignore, they make a show of patient reasonableness. Of course they welcome concerned criticism, they say. But the critic is just an amateur offering mere opinion, not scientific fact. After all, they are experts, and they know. Having said this, they go on to speak of the high professional competence of the people who make their tests. They point with pride to the elaborate scientific ritual they follow in constructing and evaluating their tests. And then, for the *coup de grâce,* they bring out their big gun—their "statistics show . . ." maneuver; by insisting that "statistics show . . .," they surround themselves with such an aura of scientific infallibility that few people realize they have avoided answering the criticism aimed at them. Then, having cleverly suggested that they are as scientific as their critics are romantic, the testers rest behind their statistical ramparts and calmly wait for the squall to pass.

The "statistics show . . ." maneuver has so powerful an effect on the layman, and even on scholars, that the test experts have come to regard it as the supreme weapon. In the battle for people's minds no general criticism can make appreciable headway against it.

If significant results are to be achieved, the critic must devise a new strategy. He must save his general criticisms till a later stage, or, at most, use them initially only in a supporting role. Instead of aiming at the central issues, he must focus on a particular weak spot in the testers' defences, find a way to turn their favorite weapons into boomerangs, and so cause the testers, in their attempts to defend themselves with improvised weapons, to expose some of their shortcomings to public view.

Not only does such a strategy exist, but it is one of

extreme simplicity: the critic merely exhibits defective multiple-choice questions, declares that they are defective, and challenges the test-makers publicly to defend these, their own questions, *specifically.*

The testers intensely dislike this sort of challenge. It puts them in a quandary. They have to be wary of conceding that the questions are bad and claiming that bad questions are rare exceptions, for they do not know how many more examples the challenger has in reserve. On the other hand, if they defend a specific bad question by their "statistics show . . ." maneuver, they risk the implication that their use of statistics is improper or that their statistics are untrustworthy; for if a question is manifestly bad, statistics can not properly prove it to be good. Again, if the testers defend the question by referring to the scientific ritual they use in constructing their tests, they undermine faith in the efficacy of that ritual and cause people to doubt that it is really as scientific as the testers would have them believe. If the testers defend a bad question by pointing to the high caliber of their staff experts and consultants they may well start people wondering whether the caliber is high enough. Therefore a sharply focused challenge to the testers to defend specific questions seems to be the one *effective* means by which the quality of multiple-choice tests can be called into question.

Since the attack is focused on what is essentially a peripheral point, it can be no more than a beginning. Its objective is merely to breach the defence, to make a prima facie case for a concentrated effort directed not merely at such peripheral points as the quality of specific questions but also, and more urgently, at the general issues that lie at the heart of the matter. What is needed for an effective frontal attack on the problem is the formation of a distinguished committee of inquiry that will look into the whole matter of testing in the United States from a fresh point of view and form a comprehensive and independent judgment in the public interest. The eminence and intellectual stature of the members of the committee must be such that its recommendations will carry impressive authority and will not go unheeded. Only through such powerful methods does there seem to be any possibility of bringing about significant reforms.

The strategy was tried out in two articles: one, entitled " 'Best' Answers or Better Minds," appeared in the Spring, 1959, issue of *The American Scholar;* the other, already referred to, was entitled "The Tyranny of Multiple-Choice Tests," and appeared in the March, 1961, issue of *Harper's Magazine.* The former exhibited the "colonies" question in the manner here presented in Chapter 1, and elicited, among other things, an official response from Henry Chauncey, the president of Educational Testing Service, which was printed, together with a rebuttal, in the Autumn, 1959, issue of *The American Scholar.* However, the official response did not defend the "colonies" question specifically. Instead, following the routine defence pattern of the professional testers, it concentrated on such matters as the efficacy of the statistical procedures by which multiple-choice tests are made, and the high caliber of the people making them, referring to the latter in these words: "Hundreds of outstanding teachers from schools and colleges work with Educational Testing Service each year to make the examinations we give as good as possible."

Few people remain unimpressed by such reassuring tactics. Few realize their essential irrelevance to the specific issue of the merits of a particular question. The public tends to believe, as it was intended to believe, that the "hundreds of outstanding teachers from schools and colleges," the pre-test statistics, and the like, somehow render the question immune to criticism, instead of being themselves on trial.

Because the initial challenge had not been met, it was repeated much more sharply in the article in *Harper's*

Magazine, where four further defective questions were exhibited, three of them made by the Educational Testing Service. This time the challenge brought forth defences of specific questions, and other revealing items, among them the response from the National Merit Scholarship Corporation that was discussed two chapters back. In succeeding chapters we give details of some of the results of the new strategy. One of the more diverting is best told here, if only in order to tell of bleak failure first. *Harper's Magazine* publishes a special edition for students which, in addition to the regular contents, contains a section, edited by university professors, that discusses the regular contents, asks questions about them, suggests topics for discussion, and so on. In the part discussing "The Tyranny of Multiple-Choice Tests," six of the questions about it were of the multiple-choice type.

Not only that, but I was not always sure myself which was the "best" answer.

Chapter 11

Critical Thinking

SUPPOSE YOU were up for promotion to an executive position and were ordered to take the *Watson-Glaser Critical Thinking Appraisal.* Your career may be at stake. In the part of the test called "Recognition of Assumptions," you read that you are *"to decide for each assumption whether it necessarily is taken for granted in the statement."* You then read the sample question, reproduced on the next page, that is intended to show what you are required to do; neither you nor the tester, of course, would provide parenthetical explanations of the choices if this were an actual instead of a sample question. The marks at the right, used for machine scoring, indicate that the "correct" answer is that Assumptions 1 and 2 are MADE, while Assumption 3 is NOT MADE.

Passing over the doubly faulty English in the phrase "greater speed of a plane over other means of transportation," look at the second proposed assumption, bearing in mind what the test is supposed to test, and note the force of the word *"necessarily"* in the italicized part of the instructions. In order to save time by plane it must indeed be possible to go by plane. But not necessarily "to our destination." Nor are plane "connections" essential. Therefore, the correct answer ought to be "not made."

159

TEST 2

	ASSUMPTION	
	MADE	NOT MADE
1	▨	:·····:
2	▨	:·····:
3	:·····:	▨

EXAMPLE. STATEMENT: "We need to save time in getting there, so we'd better go by plane."

PROPOSED ASSUMPTIONS:

1. Going by plane will take less time than going by some other means of transportation. (It is assumed in the statement that greater speed of a plane over other means of transportation will enable the group to get to their destination in less time.) ---

2. It is possible to make plane connections to our destination. (This necessarily assumed in the statement, since, in order to save time by plane, it must be possible to go by plane.) ---

3. Travel by plane is more convenient than travel by train. (This assumption is not made in the statement—the statement has to do with saving time, and says nothing about convenience or about any other specific mode of travel.) ---

* Sample question from the "Watson-Glaser Critical Thinking Appraisal," "Recognition of Assumptions" (Copyright 1951-52 by Harcourt, Brace & World, Inc.; reproduced by permission).

But the test-maker says it is "made." Thus, with your future at stake, and with resentment mounting inside you, you must now abandon logic and embark instead on the hazardous task of trying to guess what other blunders the tester has made. You dare not assume he has made none. No matter how transparent a question may seem, you must stalk it warily, wondering what possible mental quirk may have influenced the test-maker's choice of answer. And while you are agonizing over the answers, less capable competitors in the promotion race who failed to spot the error are going blithely ahead, quite possibly picking wanted answers, and certainly confident that they are taking an objective test.

What would happen if you protested? Judging by what has happened in the past when individual questions have been criticized, I believe the test experts might deny that the question was bad. Certainly, they would point out that in all the years the test had been in use nobody else had complained about the question and that, in any case, statistics proved the test to be an excellent instrument for determining who is able to think critically and who is not.

In effect, you would be told that you must pay a penalty for being exceptional. You are a statistical misfit in an age of mechanized judgment.

*   *   *

It is worth pointing out here that the above question is really just a true-false question in disguise. It can be worded:

The proposed assumption is necessarily taken for granted in the statement:
☐ True   ☐ False

The excerpt starting at the beginning of this chapter and ending at the row of asterisks is quoted verbatim* from the

---

* Except that "on the next page" replaces "below."

article in *Harper's Magazine*. Later in 1961 revised, and materially changed forms of the *Watson-Glaser Critical Thinking Appraisal* were brought out to replace the earlier forms, and in the new edition the sample question about the "plane" is significantly modified as are the directions associated with it. The present discussion pertains to the earlier edition, which is now superseded. As for the sample question reproduced above from the earlier edition, the president of Harcourt, Brace & World, Inc., William Jovanovich, agreed that it was "badly worded and confusing." However, Dr. Edward M. Glaser, co-author of the *Watson-Glaser Critical Thinking Appraisal,* sought to defend it as follows:

Regarding the criticism of the second proposed assumption, "It is possible to make plane connections to our destination" —touché on Dr. Hoffmann's proofreading! The wording of this particular assumption can be improved, but it is not nearly as bad as Dr. Hoffmann contends. Why should the word "to" mean "all the way to" instead of meaning "in the direction of?" And plane "connections" mean only from one plane to another; don't you also make connections from car to plane; or will he argue that it isn't strictly necessary to get to the airport at all—you might be born there?

I would like to leave it to each reader to decide for himself, given the wording in the sample as it stands, whether the correct answer to assumption #2 is MADE, as the test makers assert it is, or NOT MADE, which Dr. Hoffmann asserts ought to be the correct answer.

It is natural for an author of a test to wish to defend his work. But the meaning of the second assumption is plain; and if, for example, the word "to" was meant to imply merely "in the direction of," should it not, in the interests of clarity, have been replaced by some such word as "towards"? The instructions to the candidate are quite explicit. After the italicized part already quoted at the beginning of this chapter, they go on as follows, emphasizing the formerly quoted "necessarily" by repeating it: "If you think the given assumption is taken for granted in the statement, make a heavy mark between the dotted lines under 'ASSUMPTION MADE' in the proper place on the Answer Sheet. If you think the assumption is not necessarily taken for granted in the statement, make a heavy line under 'ASSUMPTION NOT MADE' on the Answer Sheet." Such instructions give the candidate little if any leeway. Yet Dr. Glaser, after conceding that the question is somewhat less than impeccably worded, chooses nevertheless to defend it, and does so by pleading for laxity in interpretation. Not only is this sort of defence unbecoming; it is also self-defeating, for its effect is to accentuate the woes of the superior candidate and to convert the test into a test of *un*critical thinking.

Chapter 12

Editorial Woes

How would you feel if, on applying for a responsible position, you were given a test with questions like this:

You are an editor forced to turn down a scholarly book which you think is a good piece of work but which will not sell. Which one of the following statements would best inform the author of your decision without discouraging him?

(A) You'll probably think me grossly mercenary when I tell you that, good though I think it is, I must turn down your book because it would have very little commercial success.

(B) You are obviously unfamiliar with the requirements of the publishing business—through no fault of your own. The point is that your book would have a very limited sale, and therefore we cannot accept it.

(C) Having read your book with great care, I must admit that it is a creditable effort. However, we doubt that it would have a great enough sale to justify our publishing it.

(D) We feel that your book is an important contribution in its field. But, since so few readers are interested in that field, we find that we cannot fit the book into our publishing program.

You cannot, of course, ask your examiner what he meant by "would best inform the author of your decision *without discouraging him."* You are not allowed to ask questions; nor even to explain your answer. You must simply pick a letter—A, B, C, or D; you will be judged right if you pick the one the tester wants, wrong if you do not. If you fail to pick the wanted answer, and thereby jeopardize your chances of getting the job, it will be small consolation to you to know that neither one of the two editors on whom I tried this question picked the right answer.

This question is a product of the Educational Testing Service. It is taken verbatim from a booklet, *Sample Questions from the Foreign Service Officer Examination,* put out by the U. S. State Department, and is quoted here with permission. It is intended to test "the candidate's ability to recognize the appropriateness of certain forms of expression to specific situations."

I tried it on several of my colleagues. Here are their choices (I omit their various cogent reasons): a professor of classics—D; a public relations man—C; a personnel director—C; a professor of music widely known for his writing ability—A; a professor of English—A; a professor of anthropology—C; two professors of anthropology acting in concert (after long wavering between A and D)— A; a professor of English—D; a dean—C. And not one of them had a kind word to say for the question. (The test-makers happen to consider answer D the best.)

Do questions of this sort really test what is claimed? Do they not rather test ability to fathom what is in the mind of the examiner?

*   *   *

The above from the start of this chapter to the row of asterisks appeared in the article in *Harper's Magazine.*

In response to that article, the Educational Testing Service, in April, 1961, issued a pamphlet with the title *Explanation of Multiple-Choice Testing,* and the parenthetical subtitle "(With particular reference to items which

have been criticized in articles by Dr. Banesh Hoffmann)."
This pamphlet contains specific defences of all those of its
questions that I had attacked publicly in print, these, at
the time, being five in number.

The defence of the above "editor" question reads as
follows:

Explanation—This question was chosen to illustrate one
of the tests in the series which is administered to candidates
for positions as Foreign Service Officers in the Department
of State. It is designed to test sensitivity to the reactions of
others to written communication. Presumably, this would be
an important quality in Foreign Service Officers. Obviously,
this is a difficult quality to measure by any means. And it
certainly can't be measured by giving a person a question
in which logic or accuracy of grammatical knowledge will
produce the correct answer. A certain amount of ambiguity
is part and parcel of this kind of test. The distinctions must
be rather small and subtle in order to have any kind of
measure at all. On any one item, even a very sensitive and
perceptive person might, by a particular line of reasoning,
give the wrong response. However, if 50 or more such questions are asked, the sensitive, perceptive person will agree,
more often than the person lacking in sensitivity, with the
answers selected by panels who have prepared the questions
following a carefully developed plan.

For example, the thinking of the panel which prepared the
item quoted above was somewhat like this:

Obviously, Option B is the least diplomatic response. A
reader might very logically interpret the statement as meaning, "You are obviously an ignoramus, but, of course, I know
that your ignorance is not your own fault."

Option A is somewhat better than Option B, but it doesn't
avoid discouraging the author; it simply permits him to
project his feeling of hopelessness in a mercenary world on
the editor. It is small comfort to know that a grossly mercenary editor *thinks* the book is good (but isn't really sure).

Option C comes closer to the mark, but in comparison

with Option D, it is clearly second best. The dollar signs are somewhat disguised ("we doubt that it would have great enough sale") and the editorial "we" is used to soften the refusal, but the response abounds in clichés which wound— without intent. The basis of judgment is put in the singular. The only person who has read the book is the writer of the letter. And having read it with great *care* (not especially suggestive of perception, and certainly not of sympathy) the *one* man *must admit* that the *effort* is *creditable*. If I say I am forced to admit, I suggest that my approach has been negative, and I really don't want to make the judgment forced upon me. As for *effort*; this suggests, "Well, anyway, you tried—but so what!" The ultimate wound is the word *creditable*; this word is reserved for the efforts of amateurs.

In contrast, Option D provides the ultimate compliment to a scholar—"an important contribution in its field"—and focuses on the limited number of people competent to appreciate the work rather than on the number of dollars they might generate for the publisher. *We* is used throughout; it may be the editorial *we,* but it does not hit the reader with the condescending tone of Option C. The author is encouraged, in a sense, to try to reach his limited audience in some other way—perhaps by microfilming the manuscript.

The Educational Testing Service attempts to make answer D seem by all odds the best. But it does so by the simple expedient of using a double standard, as we shall show. The "editor" question is, in fact, highly ambiguous, as is demonstrated by the variety of responses made by my colleagues. The only point on which there seems to be general agreement is that answer B lacks merit. For the rest, the question is so ambiguous that when I submitted the article containing it to *Harper's Magazine* without indicating which was the wanted answer, the editors found themselves utterly baffled and begged me to say which one it was.

Answer C impresses me as weak for somewhat the same reasons as those cited by ETS: "I must admit" is too grudging, and "creditable effort" damns with faint praise. Yet "we doubt that it would have a great enough sale to justify our publishing it" expresses this point far better than any of the other answers does. Indeed, it is so good that, in my view, it is out of keeping with the rest of answer C, making that answer a hybrid lacking consistency of style. Yet people whom I respect picked answer C, among them two editors associated with two different organizations. Who are the ETS committee and I to say categorically that these people are wrong, especially when no answer is free of flaws and qualified people differ as to which is the best answer?

As for myself, my initial preference was for either A or D, and for a while I could not decide between them. But the longer I considered them, the less I liked D and the more I liked A.

Despite its editorial "we," or perhaps because of it, answer D seems to me to be impersonal and unimaginative. It is made up of conventional phrases and has about it the chill air of a form letter, its non-specific wording calling up the image of a neatly printed form; note the disingenuous specificity of "in its field" and "in that field," phrases that apply to a wide variety of books. The compliment, "an important contribution in its field," is marred not only by "in its field" but also by the ill-chosen introductory phrase "We feel that," with all its infelicitous implications. See how much stronger the compliment would have been had these three words been omitted. And note how Educational Testing Service uses a double standard here. It conveniently switches its sensitivity on and off, reacting with unnecessary sharpness to the "I think" in answer A but saying not a word about the "We feel" in the answer it wishes to defend, and then, having implied by its silence that it finds "We feel" innocuous, nevertheless taking care not to include it when citing the compliment that the phrase mars.

Answer D might yet have seemed encouraging had it not ended as it does. But the phrase "cannot fit the book into our publishing program" is patently insincere; and as such it is a cliché that wounds. For the book is clearly being rejected because it will not make money, and to attempt to sweeten this blunt truth by an inappropriate and insincere cliché is not to encourage the perceptive author but to lead him to doubt the sincerity of all that has gone before—including the imperfect compliment. The perceptive author will probably conclude that answer D is a polite but routine rejection slip which, despite its seeming words of praise, carries no genuine implication that his book is good.

By way of contrast, let us now look at answer A with a friendly eye. This answer could also be a routine rejection form. But it certainly does not sound like one. It is forthright and has a warm personal touch. Moreover, it bears the imprint of a gentleman, for by altruistically suggesting that the editor is a mercenary boor, it offers the author a ready-made explanation for the rejection of his book that kindles the hope that a less mercenary editor— say, of a university press—might accept it. Above all, the editor emerges as a human being rather than a formal, disembodied "we."

There is really no pat answer to the "editor" question. Perhaps the most striking thing about the defence made by ETS is its frank admission that "a certain amount of ambiguity is part and parcel" of tests of "sensitivity to the reactions of others to written communication," and that "the distinctions must be rather small and subtle."

One would think that these basic facts argued against the use of the multiple-choice format. But the Educational Testing Service apparently believes otherwise. It would mitigate them by an essentially statistical remedy: many questions. It argues that though a very sensitive and perceptive person might give the wrong response on one particular question, he will, on the whole, do better than candidates lacking sensitivity if fifty or more such questions are asked. This is hardly convincing. It is reminiscent of the story of the manufacturer who said he lost money on each item he sold but made up for it by enormous volume of sales.

The whole subtest takes a mere hour and a quarter. If it is to be a test of sensitivity of the type that ETS defends, all the fifty or more questions—to be answered at the rate of two every three minutes or so—will presumably have to contain "a certain amount of ambiguity" and involve "rather small and subtle" distinctions. If one such question disturbs a very sensitive and perceptive person, imagine the nightmarish effect that fifty or more would have on him. There is no guarantee that he will do better on them than a less perceptive candidate will. What if he has greater sensitivity than the ETS committee? Will he not then be likely to pick consistently better answers than they do? What if he has an original, unconventional mind and does not happen to think along committee lines? Will he not then be likely, for excellent reasons, to pick answers different from those they prefer? Remember that the distinctions are "rather small and subtle."

The main function of the ETS committee's choices is to furnish a basis for "objective" scoring in a highly subjective field. Despite the existence of official "best" answers —or perhaps because of them—questions such as the "editor" question are intellectual quicksands. And when a question of this sort is exhibited in an official booklet as a sample of the questions on the Foreign Service tests, it can not but deter some of the most perceptive and most promising prospects from even applying for a position.

Chapter 13

"The wind bloweth where it listeth"

HERE IS a sentence-completion question:

22. If we cannot make the wind blow when and where we wish it to blow, we can at least make use of its

----------------.

(A) source (B) heat (C) direction
(D) force (E) atmosphere

Most of the people to whom I show this question immediately realize that (C) and (D) are possible answers. On reflection they realize that (B) is also a possible answer. If they are of a literary turn of mind, they at first see little merit in answer (A); but when I point out that to scientists the phrase "the source of the wind" implies the combination of the heat of the sun and the rotation of the earth, they look on (A) with renewed interest and often agree that it may well be the best answer. Answer (E) seems impossible: we do not usually talk of the wind's atmosphere. Yet with a little poetical license we might, and then (E) would be a doughty contender. Let us not become poetical, though. These questions are hard enough when we remain prosaic. Even without (E) there are four promising candidates.

The examiner happens to want answer (D), but unfortunately he gives no reasons for his choice. I wonder whether he noticed that the presence of the word "where" suggests (C) rather than (D) even though force has both magnitude and direction; or that it is possible to see in the phrase "at least" a further suggestion that (C) is preferable to (D), and this despite the fact that we cannot use the wind's "direction" without to some extent using its "force."

The presence of the phrase "at least" raises many problems. The sentence would have a sharper focus were "at least" deleted, especially if the first word were changed from "If" to "Although"; and I think the sense of the sentence would not be substantially affected by the change. Why, then, was "at least" inserted? Was it intended as a clue? If so, it is an obscure one, for the precise significance of "at least" in the sentence is tantalizingly elusive. Does it imply some sort of a minimum, for instance? I am not convinced that it must; but if it does, precisely what sort? Again, is "at least" meant to modify no more than "we can . . . make use of," or is some of its effect meant to spill over on to the "its . . ."? If the latter, are we supposed to use it in ranking the various answers? And if the former, would not the whole situation have been much improved had the examiner avoided ambiguity by giving the sentence the logical ending ". . . we can at least make use of it"? To be sure, this would have destroyed the question, but under the circumstances that could hardly be classed as a calamity. . . .

*   *   *

The above, from the beginning of this chapter to the row of asterisks, first appeared, through the literary hospitality of Jacques Barzun, on pages 266-7 of *The House of Intellect*. The question, like the "colonies" question, was taken from the booklet *Scholastic Aptitude Test* put out by the College Entrance Examination Board in 1956.

In its pamphlet *Explanation of Multiple-Choice Testing,* the Educational Testing Service quoted only part of the remarks quoted above concerning the "wind" question. It stopped with the words "Even without (E) there are four promising candidates," following them by a few dots and the misleading statement that "Dr. Hoffmann then proceeds to concentrate on the apparent ambiguity between choices C and D." Its official defence of the question should be read with this in mind, since it is addressed more to the person who has read the truncated quotation than to the person who has read the complete commentary. Here is the defence made by ETS.

Explanation—In the sentence-completion type of question, the task is to select the choice which is consistent in logic and style with other elements in the sentence. Repeated studies have demonstrated that individuals who are adept at handling this kind of task are likely to be successful in academic work.

With respect to the question cited above, Dr. Hoffmann himself agrees that choice E is least tenable. Further, in the context of the incomplete sentence given in this question, choices A and B can scarcely be considered to convey a sensible or meaningful completion to the idea, Dr. Hoffmann's tenuous logic notwithstanding. This is borne out by the fact that a statistical analysis of student performance on this question showed that *none* of the abler students selected either choice A or B. However, a reasonable uncertainty as to what was intended may well exist as between choices C (direction) and D (force).

The author of this question presumably considered D a superior answer to C for reasons somewhat as follows: If we do use the *direction* of the wind, we do so by *accommodating* to the direction in order to make use of its force, as by heading into the wind in landings and takeoffs at airports, sailing a boat, and turning a windmill to face the wind. In these cases the changing direction of the wind is merely a nuisance; what we are after is its force.

On the other hand, one can look at the question quite literally. It states in effect that we cannot *control* either the *time or direction* of the wind. But there is a possible case for saying that we can *at least* make *use* of the latter—namely the direction. For example, one uses a weather-vane exclusively to obtain the *direction* of the wind irrespective of whether it be of hurricane force or merely that of a light summer breeze. Hunters likewise make use of the *direction* of the wind so as to forestall detection by their prey. Since *direction* is one aspect of the physical definition of force, direction is therefore a lesser *use* of the wind than is force. Thus C (direction) might be considered to be the correct answer, and indeed several of the abler students did select this choice. However, it is significant that the abler students as a group picked choice D (the correct answer according to the author of the question) in a ratio of eight to one.

The weaknesses of this defense are clear enough. There is no need to analyse them in any detail. A few brief remarks will suffice.

Let us not pause over the dismissal of awkward points by reference to "tenuous logic" and appeal to statistics. What shall we think of an organization that fails to quote the part of the commentary that deals with the crucial question of the precise significance of the "at least," and then demonstrates that it can not make up its own mind as to the significance of that phrase? Note how, in defending answer D, the Educational Testing Service essentially rejects the idea that "at least" implies a minimal effect (in which case C would be a better answer than D), yet in defending answer C relies explicitly on the implication of a minimal effect.

One of the most remarkable aspects of this defence, though, is that after telling the merits of answer D, ETS makes an eloquent case for answer C complete with statistics that suggest that a not insignificant number of the "abler" students chose that answer. Under the circumstances, this must be regarded as an act of conspicuous courtesy, and it is only fitting that we return the courtesy by making no further comments about the defence.

Chapter 14

Return to the Colonies

HERE IS the "colonies" question once more, complete with its "entirely":

The American colonies were separate and .... entities, each having its own government and being entirely ....

(A) incomplete   —   revolutionary
(B) independent   —   interrelated
(C) unified   —   competitive
(D) growing   —   organized
(E) distinct   —   independent

Following the appearance in *The American Scholar* of the criticism of this question, as reproduced in the first chapter of this book, an important member of the staff of Educational Testing Service made a remarkable defence of the question in private correspondence. But ETS, when pressed, would not acknowledge this as its official defence; and in its official response in *The American Scholar* it avoided making any specific defence of the "colonies" question.

Spurred by the renewed and sharpened challenge in *Harper's Magazine,* the Educational Testing Service, in its pamphlet *Explanation of Multiple-Choice Testing,* at last discussed the "colonies" question specifically. But, as will be seen, it did so evasively.

Recall the feeling you had, when reading Chapter 1, that this "colonies" question was a caricature made up specially for the occasion, and that I had deliberately rendered it defective by first making it deal with the American colonies and then inserting the word "entirely." Recall, too, your feelings on learning that the question had been taken verbatim from a College Board booklet, and that the wanted answer was not D but E, with all its tautology, banality, and incorrectness. And now read what ETS offers as its official defence of the question, noting, among other things, the appeal to statistics, the misunderstanding at the end, and the failure to make any specific mention of the crucial word "entirely." The non-responsive nature of its defence makes understandable the Educational Testing Service's previous official reluctance to defend the question specifically. Here is its defence in full:

Explanation—There is little reason to believe that candidates taking the SAT develop the paranoic suspicion described by Dr. Hoffmann. Prior to taking the test, each candidate is provided with a booklet containing many sample questions. If he should, like Dr. Hoffmann, find a few with which he might disagree, the explanation accompanying each answer should reassure him that he may expect no "trick" questions. (Actually, in his several reviews, Dr. Hoffmann has shown high aptitude for choosing the "correct" answers to our questions even when his logic leads him to believe that the question is defective.) We have interviewed candidates at the end of a period of testing, and while they often indicate that they feel the test has been a difficult one, they invariably report that it seems to be "fair."

Actually, the question is relatively easy for College Board candidates. Eighty-seven percent of a representative sample gave the correct answer. It discriminates between people with high general ability and people with low ability. While some individuals did mark wrong answers, it is more likely that they fell into simple semantic errors associated with fuzzy thinking rather than that they experienced the inarticulate rage reflected in Dr. Hoffmann's description. He admits that the answer is obvious to the candidate who is free from suspicion—and who presumably has sufficient verbal ability to sort out the various options.

Detailed comment is hardly necessary. But we should not let pass the implication that multiple-choice tests are "fair." Interviewing candidates can not produce worthwhile evidence that the tests are "fair," for their views can hardly be considered well-founded: they do not know whether the answers they chose were in fact the wanted answers. Had they, for example, picked answer D on the "colonies" question in a test, they would not have known that what they considered the best answer was not the official "best," and they might well, therefore, have thought the question fair.

Perhaps the intention of ETS was not to show that the tests are fair but just to show that candidates think they are fair, and thus to refute the point that the deep students are penalized both by faulty questions themselves and by their halo effect. But when ETS says that students "invariably" regarded the tests as fair, does it intend "invariably" to mean "without exception"? Only the exceptional candidates are likely to perceive the defects in multiple-choice questions, and only the more courageous and discourteous among them are likely to speak up to the makers of the tests about the defects of the test-makers' product.

If ETS had been seriously concerned about the matter, would it have conducted so lackadaisical a research? Would it not have made an elaborate investigation of a magnitude comparable to that of its study of English composition tests? The manner in which a question is posed can greatly affect the answer. Here is a way to investigate the matter more thoroughly: rate the candidates in the usual way by means of a multiple-choice test, and then, without prior warning, give out the list of wanted answers and have the candidates re-examine the test and point out the ambiguities and errors in it.

The experiment should not be performed half-heartedly. The invitation to the candidates to exercise their critical faculties should be warmly positive, and the rewards for the most cogent sets of criticisms should be substantial—scholarships involving both money and prestige, for example.

Despite the strong inducement, the candidates might "invariably" find no defects. But suppose some candidates did find a significant number of defects. Then we can speculate on some possible outcomes of the experiment and, by so doing, begin to understand why the testers have not performed it seriously.

Suppose, for example, that there proved to be a significant tendency for the most profound critics not to be among the high scorers on the multiple-choice test. That would imply that the test was discriminating against a most important type of candidate.

Suppose that no significant pattern emerged. Then it would be clear that the multiple-choice test was failing to measure an extremely important trait that ought not to be ignored even though it might be one that the test-makers lack.

Suppose, finally, that the candidates who were the best at discovering ambiguities and errors in the test turned out to be, on the whole, those who scored highest on the test itself. If the testers claimed this as a vindication of their test, they would reveal the narrowness of their statistical outlook. For would not the experiment have demonstrated that the tests were fostering opportunism, conformism, tongue-in-cheek cynicism, and intellectual dishonesty?

Chapter 15

Interlude on the Advantages of Science

IN DEFENDING the "editor" question, the Educational Testing Service conceded the presence of ambiguity, and even sought to suggest that it was a virtue, by pointing out that a certain amount of ambiguity is part and parcel of tests of sensitivity to the reactions of others to written communication. In defending other questions, though, it does not stress this matter of the presence of ambiguity. Yet it and other test-makers are ready to plead for just enough special laxity in the interpretation of words to allow them to escape from an awkward position even though they deny the candidate equivalent latitude on the ground that the test is objective.

This particular tactic is often well concealed. But camouflaging it successfully is difficult in the case of questions on science where precision is crucial. For this reason, defective science questions make ideal challenge questions and produce particularly sharp results.

The disadvantage in the use of science questions as challenge questions is that they involve technicalities that may not be readily understood by the non-specialist. But this disadvantage is more than compensated for by the exceptional clarity with which such questions allow one to expose fuzzy thinking on the part of the test-makers, not to mention lack of relevant knowledge.

In the next two chapters, therefore, we tell about two challenge questions in science and the precise and disturbing evidence they produced concerning the quality of tests and the level of competence of test-makers.

The questions were taken from a booklet, *Science,* published in 1954 by the College Entrance Examination Board. This booklet describes science tests used by the College Board as part of its college entrance testing program, these science tests being tests not of "aptitude" but of actual achievement. The sample questions that follow give an indication of the extraordinary manner in which the College Board measures the scientific caliber of candidates for entrance to college.

Do not be deterred by the presence of unfamiliar scientific expressions. The defects in the questions and in the defences of the questions are so striking that they tower above the technical background, and scientific knowledge is not needed in order to understand their nature. If, therefore, some of the terms are obscure, simply ignore them.

Chapter 16

Einstein Slighted

HERE IS question 54 in *Science*. It is listed as belonging to chemistry and its degree of difficulty is said to be "average."

54. The burning of gasoline in an automobile cylinder involves all of the following *except*

(A) reduction
(B) decomposition
(C) an exothermic reaction
(D) oxidation
(E) conversion of matter to energy.

The average chemistry student quickly picks the wanted answer E, doubtless arguing that conversion of matter into energy refers to nuclear reactions and is thus inappropriate here.

But the student who is unfortunate enough to understand, even if only in an elementary way, what $E = mc^2$ is really about finds himself at a distinct disadvantage. He knows that in certain nuclear reactions energy is released through the breaking of nuclear bonds. He knows too that in the burning of gasoline the energy released comes from the dissociation of chemical bonds, that these chemical bonds contribute, however minutely, to the rest mass of the substances involved in the reaction, and that the released energy—all of it—comes from the diminution of this rest mass. Thus here, just as in nuclear reactions, there is "conversion of matter into energy." So the superior student correctly concludes that none of the given answers is correct.

One might try to defend the question by saying that since matter is a form of energy, answer E is tautological. But, quite apart from the fact that the wording is customary, any tautology would make E *a fortiori* valid, and thus unacceptable as an answer.

*   *   *

The above, from the start of this chapter to the row of asterisks, appeared in *Harper's Magazine*. The Educational Testing Service, in its pamphlet, defended it as follows:

Explanation—The superior student is as aware of the *classical* concepts of matter and chemical change as he is of the model of *modern* physics. He is likely to be more aware than is the average student that the "conversion of matter into energy" has been demonstrated only for nuclear changes. Perhaps he realizes that if the energy freed by the burning of gasoline comes from the conversion of mass to energy, the loss in mass is only about a ten-billionth of the mass of the gasoline burned, a loss too small to be measured by available methods.

When such a student is faced with the above question, he should realize that the classical concepts of matter and chemical change provide the framework in which the question is asked. He also recognizes that the first four processes listed are obviously and immediately involved in the burning of gasoline, and he selects response E as the required answer.

How good is this defence? Not at all as good as it may seem at first sight to the non-specialist.

Note, for example, the curious implication of the words

I emphasize in this passage: ". . . the 'conversion of matter into energy' has been demonstrated ONLY for nuclear changes. Perhaps he realizes that IF the energy freed by the burning of gasoline comes from the conversion of mass to energy. . . ." Are they not intended to suggest that there is reasonable doubt that $E = mc^2$ applies to chemical as well as to nuclear processes? Does one not receive the impression that, in order to defend its question, ETS is prepared, if necessary, to abandon $E = mc^2$?

Again, the remark that the loss of mass is "too small to be measured by available methods" may well impress the non-specialist, yet it is incorrect as stated. The mass can be measured by measuring the amount of energy released and using Einstein's formula, $E = mc^2$. Even if it were true, the remark would hardly be relevant to the crucial question here of whether mass is or is not converted into energy in the burning of gasoline. Can ETS produce a competent physicist or chemist who would risk his reputation by denying in public that, according to current concepts, ALL of the released energy comes from the conversion of rest mass? If ALL the released energy comes from this conversion, the process is certainly not a negligible one here, though ETS would have us think otherwise.

Having tried to undermine $E = mc^2$, ETS next tries a different tack. Implicitly admitting the validity of $E = mc^2$, it says that the superior student "should realize that the classical concepts of matter and chemical change provide the framework in which the question is asked." Einstein's formula, $E = mc^2$, is over fifty years old. Why should the superior student realize that he is to use only those concepts that ETS chooses to regard as "classical"?

We now come to a crucial question: why was the non-"classical," relativistic answer included among the choices? Was this answer put there deliberately, or was ETS at the time it framed the question unaware of the meaning of $E = mc^2$?

Note how damaging are the implications if we assume, as perhaps ETS wishes us to, that ETS was fully aware of the meaning of $E = mc^2$ and deliberately included answer E nevertheless. For we must then ask: what was its motive for doing so? To make a question with no correct answer? Let us hope not. Then what? To penalize the superior student? One doubts that ETS would say so; yet the question is surely easier for the student who does not understand $E = mc^2$ than for the student who does. Is the latter student supposed to compensate for the deficiencies of the test-maker by reading possibly hazardous amendments into the question as worded—into a science question, moreover? That way lies chaos, not "objectivity." If the superior student does decide to pick answer E, does he not do so with contempt for the test-maker, and with cynical disregard of scientific facts? Should he be rewarded for his willingness to place expediency above scientific integrity? If tests are training students to respond in this way, are they not having a deleterious effect on education?

Perhaps, after all, it is more charitable to assume that ETS was ignorant of the meaning of $E = mc^2$ when it framed the question, even if this does imply a certain lack of candor on its part now.

Chapter 17

Light on the Atom

So MUCH for what the College Board conceives to be a question that is neither easy nor difficult but average. Here is a question that it regards as "difficult." It is question 65 and belongs to physics. The student is supposed to select the statement which gives the correct scientific cause.

65. Potassium metal loses electrons when struck by light (the photoelectric effect) more readily than lithium metal because

(A) the potassium atom contains more protons than does that of lithium

(B) the valence electron of potassium is farther from the nucleus than is that of lithium

(C) potassium occurs above lithium in the electro-chemical series

(D) the potassium atom contains more electrons than does that of lithium

(E) the potassium nucleus is larger than that of lithium

The wanted answer is B. Let us accept it as a factually correct answer and ask whether it is the best answer. We shall find that three of the other possible answers are not only factually correct statements in themselves but could be defended as more satisfactory answers than B.

Let us put ourselves in the place of a well-prepared and inquiring student faced with answer B. Yes, he may say to himself, the sentence in question can be plausibly completed with the statement that the "valence electron of potassium is farther from the nucleus than that of lithium." But he then sees that answer D accurately (if ungrammatically) states the reason *why* this is so, namely that "the potassium atom contains more electrons than does that of lithium." Thus, the student may sensibly conclude that while B is a correct answer, D is a correct answer too. And D is a more profound answer than B.

But our student is not finished. For he realizes that the reason why there are more electrons in the potassium atom than in the lithium atom is to be found in answer A: the atom of potassium "contains more protons than does that of lithium." Thus, if D is a correct answer, so is A. And A cuts deeper than D.

Finally he hesitates to dismiss E, knowing that the nucleus of potassium "is larger than that of lithium" because it contains more neutrons and protons. Thus if A is a correct answer, so also is E.

In view of the above, most of us would agree with the College Board that the question is "difficult." But with us this is merely a matter of opinion. With the test experts it is an objective, scientific, no-nonsense fact based on statistics. Of course, the statistics do not reveal that the wording of the question is vague. Nor that, if the wanted answer is a correct one, so are three others. Nor that the examiners have chosen the most immediate and superficial answer, thus penalizing the candidates with more probing minds, as they so often do. Can we be complacent when we know that such questions are used by so many of our colleges to assess scientific talent?

*   *   *

The preceding, from the start of this chapter to the row of asterisks, appeared in *Harper's Magazine*. One error needs to be corrected: the question was actually listed by the College Board as belonging to chemistry, and not to physics as stated above and in *Harper's Magazine*.

In its pamphlet, the Educational Testing Service offers a long defence of this question. Though it is not addressed solely to the specialist, it is inevitably rather technical. Read it through nevertheless. It is written with such an air of reasoned confidence and scientific logic that the non-specialist will feel convinced that it is a devastating rebuttal of an utterly base and utterly baseless criticism. Yet in fact, as will be demonstrated, it is so gravely damaging to ETS that that organization would far better have kept silent and allowed the challenge to stand against it unanswered. Here, in full, is the defence offered by ETS:

Explanation—The technical terms must be considered in studying this question. The photoelectric effect is exhibited by an element if, in atoms of the element, an electron is so loosely bound that visible light provides enough energy to free that electron from its atom. Since electrons are negatively charged, most of them are too strongly attracted to the positively charged atomic nucleus to be freed by light. The farther from the nucleus an electron is found, the more likely it is that light will be able to free the electron and that the photoelectric effect will be observed.

Since the outer—or valence—electron of a potassium atom, on the average, is farther from the nucleus than the valence electron of a lithium atom, of these two the element that shows the photoelectric effect is potassium. Response B, the accepted response to this question, is based on this reasoning.

Dr. Hoffmann agrees to accept response B and then begins to study other responses to see whether they can account for B. He reasons that if B is the cause of the photoelectric effect and if D is the cause of B, then D must be the cause of this effect.

Cause-effect relations in science are difficult to reduce to the confines of one response to a multiple-choice question; to find a chain of causes, such as Dr. Hoffmann proposes, in a single question would be most surprising, but we must look.

It is quite true that if one limits his consideration to a family of elements, like the one that contains potassium and lithium, the greater the number of electrons in an atom, the farther from the nucleus is the outer electron likely to be found. Is there a cause-effect relation here? Potassium has 19 electrons, calcium has 20; yet the outer electron of the calcium atom, on the average, is closer to the nucleus than is the valence electron of potassium. Indeed, of the elements whose atoms have progressively more electrons than potassium, krypton, with 36 electrons, is the first element for whose atoms the outer electron is normally farther from the nucleus than is the valence electron of a potassium atom. A larger number of electrons in an atom clearly does not "cause" the outer electron of an atom to be farther from its atomic nucleus. If D does not "cause" B, it can hardly be said to "cause" the photoelectric effect. The other responses cited by Dr. Hoffmann as "causes" of the effect can be criticized in the same fashion.

This is a remarkable defence, well worth examination in detail because of what it reveals of both the caliber and the tactics of ETS.

When ETS says that "the photoelectric effect is exhibited . . . if . . . an electron is so loosely bound that *visible* light provides enough energy to free that electron . . . ," and, later, that ". . . of these two [potassium and lithium] the element that shows the photoelectric effect is potassium," there is no escaping the conclusion that it believes not only that the photoelectric effect is confined to visible light, but also that the effect is not exhibited by lithium.

These are incredibly elementary blunders. And, apparently because of them, ETS does not even understand what its own question is about. It clearly believes here that its question asks for the cause of the photoelectric effect. The evidence is conclusive. Note the context of this sentence at the end of the second paragraph of its defence: "Response B, the accepted response . . . is based on this reasoning." Note, too, the words: "He reasons that if B is *the cause of the photoelectric effect* and if D is the cause of B then D must be *the cause of this effect*," "If D does not 'cause' B, it can hardly be said to *'cause' the photoelectric effect*," and "The other responses cited by Dr. Hoffmann as *'causes' of the effect*. . . ."

Now, of course, I did not cite responses as causes of the photoelectric effect as ETS asserts. I addressed myself to the actual question, not to what ETS imagined the question to be. Both potassium and lithium exhibit the photoelectric effect, as any competent chemist or physicist knows, and the question asks why "potassium metal loses electrons when struck by light (the photoelectric effect) MORE READILY than lithium metal." Does ETS expect the superior student to read possibly hazardous amendments into this question too? How can the superior student hope to guess what is in the examiner's mind when the examiner makes so many unpredictable blunders?

All this is only the beginning; there is worse to come. For example, despite what ETS says, answer B, the answer it defends, does not give the cause of the photoelectric effect.

Nevertheless, we must ask whether answer B is a good answer to the question as worded. There are many technical objections that could be made about the question, but they would be of limited interest, and we shall pass over them. Even so a few words of explanation are necessary. The crucial quantity is not distance from the nucleus but the amount of energy needed to remove the electron from the metal, and this depends in a quite complicated way on the state of the metal. Let us, for the sake of argument, assume, as ETS seems to do, that we are dealing with individual atoms, as in the gaseous state. This brings a considerable simplification. But still the amount of energy needed to remove the electron is not related in a simple way to the distance of the electron from the nucleus. There is, however, a qualitatively simple relationship when one confines oneself, for example, to the family of so-called alkali metals, to which lithium and potassium belong. Since the question pertains specifically to lithium and potassium one can therefore, for the gaseous state, make a plausible case for the relevance of answer B. Even so, B would not be a direct answer such as ETS apparently believes it to be. It would be a link in "a chain of causes" of which a more immediate link would involve the amounts of energy needed to remove the respective electrons.

So much for the scientific background. Let us now look at the maneuver by which ETS seeks to convince the reader that though answer B is acceptable, answers D, A, and E are not.

The maneuver is a simple one: by speaking loosely of "the valence electron" and "the outer electron," ETS enlarges the scope of the question by suggesting that it applies to several elements, and not just to lithium and potassium. Using this enlargement of scope, ETS denies that answer B is a consequence of answer D; that is, ETS denies that the fact that the valence electron of potassium is farther from the nucleus is a consequence of the fact that the potassium atom contains more electrons. It cites the fact that though the calcium atom has more electrons than potassium its "outer" electron is essentially closer to its nucleus. And it triumphantly points out that "of the elements whose atoms have progressively more electrons than potassium [which has only 19], krypton, with 36 electrons, is the first element of whose atoms the 'outer' electron is normally farther from the nucleus than is the valence electron of potassium."

This seems like a superb triumph. But the triumph proves illusory, for the argument boomerangs. If ETS wishes to claim that answer B is valid *when the scope of the question is enlarged* it must, from the wording of answer B, believe that the farther an electron is from the nucleus the more readily it escapes from the atom when struck by light. But, as ETS itself points out, the "outer" electron of krypton is normally farther away from the nucleus than is the valence electron of potassium. This being so, how does ETS propose to account for the awkward fact that krypton does *not* lose electrons when struck by light more readily than the potassium atom does?

ETS can not have it both ways. To make answer B acceptable it must limit the number of elements involved, in which case it can not legitimately deny that answer D causes answer B, and that A causes D. In denying that D causes B it allows many types of elements to enter, but in that case its triumphant argument against answer D destroys its own case for answer B and shows that no answer is valid.

Having observed the quality of the defences that the Educational Testing Service offered of specific challenge questions, let us now look at the setting in which the defences were given. In its pamphlet *Explanation of Multiple-Choice Testing,* it prefaced its specific defences by a preamble ending with these words: "In the sections which follow, illustrative questions which have been criticized by Dr. Banesh Hoffmann are presented, together with the detailed reasons which convinced panels of judges that they were good questions."

This sentence takes on a piquant quality when read as postscript rather than preamble.

Similarly, when the rest of the preamble is presented as postscript its piquancy too is enhanced, and we introduce it with the remark that of the three "major virtues of multiple-choice tests" that are cited, the second and third do not pertain exclusively to multiple-choice tests:

There is a strange paradox, that along with the steadily increasing use and improvement of multiple-choice tests over the past 40 years, and with the greater acceptance of them by knowledgeable people, there continue to be occasional violent attacks on the tests from what should be relatively informed sources. Apparently, these attacks stem from a distorted view of the nature of multiple-choice tests. The critics appear to focus on certain minor virtues of the tests—that they can be scored clerically or by machine and that they are relatively inexpensive—and then to assume that these virtues are obtained at the cost of more fundamental values. Actually, this is not the case.* Multiple-choice tests have gained acceptance primarily because of mounting evidence that they provide more accurate information about the abilities and achievements of individuals than can be obtained by other procedures.

The major virtues of multiple-choice tests are three. First, in a given amount of time, more questions can be asked than when the student has to write out answers to questions. This permits a much wider sampling of the subject matter, and it means that if a student, for one reason or another, does not do himself justice on one, two, or even half a dozen questions, he will not seriously affect his score.

Second, a test can be planned, and each individual question prepared with the greatest possible care. At Educational Testing Service, an achievement test is ordinarily prepared by a committee of leading scholars and teachers in the field. They develop the blueprint for the examination, the skills to be measured, and the content to be covered. They also write

* Not all laymen nor all test experts would agree with this categorical assertion. For example, individually administered Stanford-Binet IQ tests, which are not of the multiple-choice type, require the psychologists who administer them to use their judgment in scoring novel responses, and Professors Lewis W. Terman and Maud A. Merrill, in their book *Stanford-Binet Intelligence Scale* (Boston: Houghton Mifflin, 1960), have this to say on page 56: "While one could wish that the Binet scales were entirely free from subjectivity of scoring, this limitation is the price that is paid for its greater flexibility and richness as compared with tests which are stencil-scored. The price is not excessive in view of the greater psychological insight that the Binet-type of test affords."

the individual questions, review each other's questions, and in the final stages of preparation, put together the best combination of questions to comprise the total test.

The third asset that multiple-choice tests have is that they can be studied systematically. Preliminary tests using the questions that have been prepared can be tried out on students to determine whether, in fact, each individual question discriminates between the better and poorer students or whether there is an element of ambiguity in the question which harms its effectiveness. Such questions can be eliminated or revised in such a way as to avoid ambiguity.

Because of the care with which the individual questions and the total test is constructed, because of the thorough tryout that each individual question is put through, and because a large number of questions are included in each test, such tests have proved remarkably effective, both in judging a student's competence in a given field of study, and in predicting his future success. This is not to say that they are perfect or that they get at all of the qualities that it would be desirable to measure, but, to a remarkable extent, the technique has been developed so as to get at some of the higher intellectual skills that are the main ends of education.

In selecting questions for publication as illustrations, Educational Testing Service has typically selected only questions which have passed through the process described above. It is unlikely, then, that a published question will contain serious flaws—although the possibility of a defective question being overlooked still exists. What is more likely is that a particular question may be given a highly individualistic interpretation by a particular critic.

Chapter 18

David and Goliath

WHAT HAPPENS when a person complains about particular test questions depends, of course, on the circumstances. While the result is rarely encouraging, it can nevertheless be illuminating. In this chapter we present a particular case history. For reasons that will appear, the presentation must be a detailed one, yet even so it must contain some loose ends.

On March 18, 1961, a high school student wrote to the Educational Testing Service as follows:

I would like to call attention to question 33, Section 3 of the English Composition Test given March 18 at Bethesda, Maryland. The question is a sentence with four words or phrases underlined and the fifth alternative is "no error." My concern is that I did not know whether you intended for the testee to judge the "where" incorrect or if you intended that the sentence should mean that the reader (of the newspaper) learned the location of the fishermen's plight. The later came to mind first, but then I was plagued by the thought that "they" wouldn't put in something like that. On my answer sheet I indicated the former answer (hope it was right!), but I am uncertain of what was intended.

There was another question of the same type in the same

test, in which the propriety of contractions in "formal writing," a rather arbitrary descision, would have seemed to have made a difference in the answer (can't was involved, I think I answer E—no error—but can't remember for sure).

I am sad to say that March's English Composition Test seemed to support Mr. Hoffmann's article in Harper's of the same month.

I hope you will make all possible efforts to avoid such confusion in the future. In general I find you test very good (6 time veteran) and usually even informative. Seriously, I enjoy taking them.

The student received no reply. But he was made of stern stuff. He was not one to be put off by silence. On April 24, he wrote me the following letter:

I join you in complaining about the Educational Testing Service's inadequate defense, when asked, of their questions.

On March 18, 1961 I noticed two ambiguous questions on the English Composition Exam. I wrote to them on that same day and haven't heard from them since. I am also sending them a copy of this letter hoping to elicit at least an acknowledgement. I may have to send it registered mail, but I intend to get my ackowledgement!

The questioned question was specifically number 33, of part III on the Exam given at Bethesda, Maryland. It was a sentence with several parts underlined and numbered. The testee was instructed to select the underlined part, by number, which made the sentence incorrect, or a choice labelled none if the sentence was correctly written.

John read in the newspaper where three men had been stranded on an ice floe. 2   none
    5

There were three other underlined words or phrases which were irrelevant. I felt while taking the test that the sentence was correct as written, but later wondered if the E.T.S. intended that the "where" should be considered incorrect. My justification at the time was that it was very probable that John had read the location of the unfortunate incident. This question was not part of the experimental morning tests but on the afternoon Achievement exam.

On the same day that he wrote this letter to me, the student sent a copy of it to Mr. Chauncey, the president of the Educational Testing Service, together with the following letter:

I am writing to you directly because my letter to the Educational Testing Service, itself, seems to have gone unanswered. The earlier letter (March 18) concerned two questions on March 18, 1961's English Composition Exam given at Bethesda Chevy Chase High School in Bethesda, Maryland. The question is 33, of part III of the test.

Rather than go through the whole explanation again I am enclosing a copy of my letter to Dr. Hoffmann or if you wish you can search for my original letter. Also I would like to request an explanation of III 33, such as is advertised in paragraph two of your letter to *Harper's,* if available

Let us pause at this stage to examine the merits of the question as it was recollected by the student. The directions for these questions explain that "many of the sentences contain examples of word choice, usage, grammar, or idiom not consistent with the standards of formal written English," and call on the examinee to select the "unsatisfactory word or phrase" if any. We have to ask ourselves, therefore, whether the sentence

John read in the newspaper where three men had been stranded on an ice floe

is satisfactory or not.

Replacing "where" by "that" would certainly make it satisfactory. So would replacing "where" by "how," or by "why." But actually the sentence is also satisfactory as it stands, as is clear from the following slightly redundant dialogue:

"John told me that three men had been stranded on an ice floe in the Bering Strait."

"I don't believe him. How did John know where three men had been stranded on an ice floe?"

"John read in the newspaper where three men had been stranded on an ice floe."

Our first thought, in view of this, may well be that the question is ambiguous. But, of course, it is not ambiguous at all. There is only one correct answer, and that is that the sentence is satisfactory as it stands. If I say "Paul is fat," that is a correct English sentence even if I meant to say "Paul is thin." What the examiner *intended* his sentence to mean is irrelevant to the question of whether the sentence he actually wrote was a satisfactory sentence or not in its own right. For example, suppose that the sentence on the test had been

The White House gets more rare items

and the wanted answer had been to the effect that "more rare" was unsatisfactory since it should have been "rarer." Then the wanted answer would have been incorrect. The sentence is satisfactory as it stands, and it means precisely what it says. In fact, it appeared, except for the initial "the," as a headline in *The New York Times* on January 1, 1962, and the story beneath it had to do with gifts and loans to the White House of rare historic furnishings and art pieces, more of which had just been received. There is no ambiguity at all as to the meaning of the sentence— unless one assumes that the writer of the sentence was illiterate, or one is oneself illiterate.

Much the same holds for the "ice floe" sentence. It is a satisfactory English sentence, and it means precisely that John discovered the *location* of the incident by reading the newspaper. "Where three men had been stranded on an ice floe" is not like "where twice two is four." It has strong connotations of location and confirms that the "where" means just what it says. The fact that illiterate people, wishing to convey that "John read in the newspaper *that* . . . ," sometimes say "John read in the newspaper *where . . . ,*" does not make the sentence unsatisfactory. It is irrelevant. If the examiner says that the word "where" makes the sentence unsatisfactory, he is not picking a best answer, or even an acceptable alternative answer to an ambiguous question, but a clearly wrong answer to a strictly unambiguous question. Let us bear this in mind as we read on.

We have told how the student waited five weeks without receiving a reply to his initial letter to Educational Testing Service. His letter of April 24 to the president of ETS, with its accompanying copy of the letter he wrote to me, brought a relatively quick response. The student received a letter, dated May 2, 1961, from a high official of Educational Testing Service—not the president—and I received a copy of it from the high official together with thermofax copies of the student's letters quoted above. The letter that the high official wrote to the student reads as follows:

We have your letter of April 24 addressed to Mr. Chauncey and also your letter of March 18 addressed to Educational Testing Service. Thank you for giving us your reactions to two of the questions on the test.

I am sure you will understand that we cannot discuss directly in a letter the answers to questions which appear in test forms which may be used periodically, although we shall certainly see that your comments are placed before the Committee of Examiners in English Composition when they meet to carry on their work. I fear, however, that they will disagree with you regarding the ambiguity of the two questions. In fact, the difficulty you experienced with the questions was exactly that anticipated when the test was originally constructed.

We recognize that there are sometimes questions which present real ambiguities to people with a firm grasp of the principles underlying a question. However, in *good* multiple-choice questions, the problem is to construct answers which will look right to individuals who have not mastered the principles being tested. Since we are testing over a great range of ability, there will always be some individuals who have just enough knowledge to see possibilities in more than one answer and not enough knowledge to decide which is really correct. Such individuals will get some questions correct and others wrong; they will make higher scores than the individuals who have little knowledge and lower scores than individuals with much knowledge. Apparently, you are one of those borderline people with respect to the two questions about which you have written.

I trust this explanation will be helpful. The fact that you "enjoy" taking our tests suggests that you have seldom found yourself in the "boarderline" group.

Testers do not usually make such frank statements to the layman about the attitude and aims of the constructor of "*good* multiple-choice questions."

If the question was worded as the student reported, and if the examiners believed that the word "where" makes the sentence unsatisfactory, would it not seem that the examiners themselves are "individuals who have just enough knowledge to see possibilities in more than one answer and not enough knowledge to decide which is really correct"?

The high official's letter is not without smirking overtones, and these were emphasized by the following note, addressed to me, that was handwritten by the high official on the copy he sent me of the above letter:

I'm sure you'll find the attached copies of letters an interesting addition to your file of examples of the relationship— or lack of relationship—between the ability to identify ambiguity in multiple-choice questions and other desirable abilities—such as the ability to write clearly and correctly.

On receiving the above material, I wrote to the high official, on May 6, requesting permission to quote from it. And, by coincidence, the student, on the same day, wrote the following letter to the high official and sent me a copy:

At the risk of sounding sour-grapeish, I would like to point out that your apparent attitude in the letter of May 2, is exactly what Mr. Hoffmann complains about—arrogance and unwillingness to discuss the disputed issues. In this case I feel that I know what you are trying to test with the questioned sentence but I think that number 33 of part three is a poor way to do it.

Also your failure to answer my comments until prodded by what I consider a rude letter, that of April 24, is a tell-tale affirmation of the doubts which have been cast upon the reputation of the Educational Testing Service.

The student had no objection to my quoting from this correspondence and gave me permission forthwith. The high official, however, considered the matter for some months. Then, on August 7, 1961, he wrote a letter to the student and another to me. In his letter to me he demurred at permitting quotation out of context but granted permission to quote the whole correspondence provided it included his simultaneous letter to the student, of which he enclosed a copy. So lengthy a chain of correspondence might well have proved too long for full quotation in a magazine article. Fortunately it is not too long to form a chapter in a book.

Here is the letter that the high official sent to the student on August 7:

Your letter of May 6 was not ignored—though you have every reason to think it might have been since you have had no reply. Actually, the letter has given me considerable cause for thought, since it indicates a basic misunderstanding regarding the unwillingness of ETS to discuss answers to questions in active test forms. Unfortunately, if we were to engage in lengthy correspondence with every candidate who writes us, it would be impossible to offer the College Board tests at the current fees. A few minutes thought should convince you that if even a small fraction of the 139199 candidates who took the SAT in March were to write in and if each were given the same amount of professional time which your letters have received, the cost of the test would have to be increased.

We do, however, answer all original inquiries. Sometimes other duties may delay a reply, as was the case with your first letter—it was not the prodding by what you consider a "rude" letter which insured a reply to your first letter, though the "rude" letter did lead me to find it in the pending file of a busy test development associate—but we try to acknowledge all correspondence eventually. We do not ordinarily engage in extended correspondence, but your letter of May 6 indicated a failure in communication which I feel the need to explore personally. Thus, I am taking time on a Sunday afternoon in August to write you again.

It is not arrogance and unwillingness to discuss disputed issues which prevent me from explaining in detail which of two answers to a question on one of our English examinations was considered correct. To do so would mean that the test of which it is a part could not be used again and the cost of construction would be lost. Of course, if the question were really defective, then we should retire the test form and construct another which did not contain the defective question. But consider the circumstances. A secondary school senior, remembering more or less vaguely a question which was one of about 100 in a test he took in one hour in March says that the question was defective. On the other hand, three specialists in English at Educational Testing Service say the question is not defective. Five members of the College Board Committee of Examiners in English, all of whom are considered to be competent teachers of English, say that the question is not defective. When we administered the question experimentally prior to putting it into the test, the students who marked the answer you think might be right were clearly inferior to those who marked the answer we intended to be the right one.

In other words, all of the evidence we have suggests that the explanation I gave in my letter of May 2 is the valid one. If confidence in the validity of testing procedure, based as it is on such an accumulation of evidence, seems to be arrogance, what does one call confidence in the judgment that a question is ambiguous, based on personal experience in a test situation? Working as we do, with the critical eye of highly qualified committee members on us and with the spotlight of statistical analysis focused to light up each defect in our work, the professional staff at ETS has learned to place little confidence in unsupported personal judgment. In fact, humility and a willingness to accept evidence is absolutely essential to satisfactory adjustment in this work.

For all its initial politeness, this is a hard-hitting letter. Indeed, the tactics employed in it would, under other circumstances, have been overwhelming. What chance would a high school student normally have against the confident announcement that three specialists in English at Educational Testing Service and five members of the College Board Committee of Examiners in English say that the question is not defective, especially when this is coupled with the implication that his recollection of the question is significantly faulty?

The latter implication is cleverly worded: "a secondary school senior, remembering more or less vaguely a question which was one of about 100 in a test he took in one hour in March says that the question is defective."

Note how the phrase "in March" appearing in a letter written in August could well suggest to the unwary not only that the student did not jot down his recollection of the question and its number when these were fresh in his mind, but even that he is in some obscure way to blame for the long delays in answering his letters.

The student's first letter, which has here been quoted verbatim, was a hastily handwritten note. In it he said that he took the test on March 18, the very day on which he wrote the letter. And in his typewritten letter to Mr. Chauncey on April 24 he reiterated that his earlier letter had been written on the day he took the test. These facts were, of course, known to the high official.

In view of the implication that the student's recollection of the question was significantly faulty, it seemed desirable to obtain a clear statement on the matter. Accordingly I wrote to the high official asking whether the student's version of the question was in all essential respects accurate, and whether the wanted answer implied that the word "where" was incorrect. But the high official preferred not to give me any further information.

Fortunately a letter to the College Entrance Examination Board brought the information I desired; but it was given in confidence. However, I am permitted to say that I have seen the actual question.

Under the circumstances, let us look once more at the high official's letters. The implication that the student did not recall the question with essential accuracy appears in the August letter. It is best read in conjunction with the following statement in the high official's first letter to the student: "In fact the difficulty you experienced with the two questions was exactly that anticipated when the test was constructed."

What of the three specialists in English at Educational Testing Service and the five members of the College Board Committee of Examiners in English? In view of what has appeared in previous chapters, it should not be regarded as entirely inconceivable that they could, despite their unanimity, be mistaken.

Chapter 19

Don't Be Pro-Test—Protest

THE EDUCATIONAL TESTING SERVICE is the leading educational test-making organization in America. Its prestige is of the highest, its influence enormous. Its multiple-choice tests are generally recognized—and deservedly so—as among the very best being made. If, in these pages, ETS shows up as leaving something to be desired, this in no way reflects on its relative standing among test-making organizations, which remains as high as it always has been.

I have focused the main attack on the Educational Testing Service for a reason that is complimentary to that organization: one makes the strongest case by criticizing the best test-makers, not the worst. Observing the comportment of leading test-makers, can we feel confident that testing is in the best possible hands? If sample questions made by the best test-makers can give cause for concern, what of multiple-choice tests made by lesser organizations? And what of multiple-choice tests made by individual teachers for their own classroom use in the belief that they are being scientific and objective?

Some defenders of multiple-choice tests have sought to argue that the tests are on the whole quite good, so that the critic has to seek far and wide to glean a few isolated defective questions—and then only sample questions. But the use of sample questions is largely dictated by the understandable reluctance of test-makers to allow publication of actual test questions; and it makes the case against the tests stronger, not weaker—unless the test-makers would have us believe that they deliberately choose sample questions that are on the whole worse than the general run of questions in their tests. Let us recall that in the preamble of its pamphlet, *Explanation of Multiple-Choice Testing,* Educational Testing Service, after explaining how its test questions are subjected to a thorough screening process, says, "In selecting questions for publication as illustrations, Educational Testing Service has typically selected only questions which have passed through the process described above. It is unlikely, then, that a published question will contain serious flaws—although the possibility of a defective question being overlooked still exists." Through the courtesy of ETS I was permitted, a few years ago, to study an actual *Scholastic Aptitude Test* of the College Entrance Examination Board. Naturally, I may not reveal its contents; but I may record my opinion that the booklet *Scholastic Aptitude Test,* from which, for example, the "colonies" question was taken, gave a flattering rather than an unflattering portrayal of the tests it described.

The matter of testing has many ramifications, of which the existence of manifestly defective multiple-choice questions in even the best of tests is by no means the most important. Nevertheless the fact that such questions exist is embarrassing to the testers, and they seek at times to belittle its significance by using such terms as "nit-picking" and by suggesting that defective questions are few and far between. But in fact the defects are anything but trifling, as we have seen, and the number of defective questions is by no means negligible. Indeed defective questions are quite readily come by. One does not have to scour the countryside for them in desperate search. One has but to shake the tree and they fall in abundance. Anticipating the objection that defective questions are relatively scarce, I prepared, a few years ago, a list of twelve challenge questions taken from the two College Board booklets, *Scholastic Aptitude Test* and *Science*, already cited, among the twelve being the "colonies" question, the "wind" question discussed in Chapter 13, and the two science questions discussed in Chapters 16 and 17. These twelve questions constitute 5 per cent of the questions in the booklets, a percentage that should give us pause, especially when we recall that the questions were culled from official samples used to indicate the nature of the tests to the prospective candidate, and somehow to "reassure him that there are no 'trick' questions."

That 5 per cent and more of the sample questions in two booklets should be defective is sufficiently disquieting in itself. Yet the situation is worse than it appears to be, for a simple percentage gives a misleading idea of the impact of the defective questions even apart from the fact that a percentage takes no account of the considerable halo effect of these questions. For example, suppose that a test had a hundred questions of which 50 are of a trivially routine sort dealing with superficial items of fact, vocabulary, and the like. Because of the very nature of the multiple-choice format, the defective questions are apt to be found among the other 50 questions that are intended to be more searching. If there are 5 defective questions among these latter, though they constitute 5 per cent of the total they are effectively 10 per cent so far as the rankings of the better students are concerned.

There is more to the selection of the twelve challenge questions than the overall percentage indicates. Five of the twelve are of the sentence-completion type, and since there were only twenty-one sample questions of that type to choose from, these five questions constitute 24 per cent of the supply. Worse, in the booklet *Science* there were only three sample questions classified as dealing with "ability to interpret cause and effect relationships." One of the three was said to be of average difficulty, the other two being labelled "difficult." One of these two "difficult" questions is the "potassium" question discussed in Chapter 17, and both of the "difficult" questions are included in the list of twelve challenge questions. For those who like to play with percentages and stretch statistics we mention that these two questions, taken from a total of three, constitute over 66 per cent of questions of the type, and thus emphasize that in multiple-choice tests difficulty is too often achieved by means of ambiguity.

As we have already explained, objection to the presence of defective questions in multiple-choice tests, albeit serious, is merely peripheral. It does, however, serve the purpose of forcing the test-makers to come out into the open. And this exposure, in addition to having a telling effect on specialist and layman alike, provides solid evidence which makes a clear prima facie case for the setting up of a distinguished committee of inquiry. Causing test-makers to defend their samples has had a result that the test-makers may not fully have appreciated: it has significantly broadened the base of the prima facie case. The case no longer rests solely on the question of the quality of the samples presented here; it now embraces also the question of the quality of the test-makers and the nature of their tactics. In its pamphlet *Explanation of Multiple-Choice Testing,* for example, the Educational Testing Service clearly tries to give the layman the impression that the criticized sample questions are good. It does not say "Oops. Sorry!" It brazens the matter out. Such conduct is disturbing in itself: no matter how well it may accord with acceptable standards of behavior in business, politics, propaganda, and the cold war, it is unbecoming in a test-making organization that would have the public regard it as objective and scientific. But, as we have seen, the specific result of this conduct has been to contribute even more strongly to the prima facie case. For by its maladroit defence of the "gasoline" question, for example, ETS lays itself open, by implication, to the charge that it deliberately used a "wanted" answer that would trouble the students who understood $E=mc^2$. And in defending the "potassium" question it makes blunders of a nature that must give rise to serious concern.*

In fairness, let me reiterate that I focus the main attack on ETS because of its pre-eminence in the field of academic testing. There is no reason at all to suppose that other academic test-making organizations would prove to be any the less vulnerable, and no implication that their tests are necessarily better than those made by ETS. For salesmen of rival tests to suggest otherwise on the basis of the evidence presented here would certainly be improper.

When testers are faced with general criticisms they are apt to pooh-pooh them as mere expressions of opinion, much as they do the resolutions, passed hopefully by organizations of teachers, that urge greater use of essay tests because of the deleterious effects multiple-choice tests have on education. Essay tests are not as bad as the test psychologists would have us believe—nor multiple-choice tests as good. Countries like Denmark, England, France, and Russia, to name but four, use essay tests extensively. And we may note, not without wry amusement, that the professional examinations for the Diplomate in Psychology, consisting, as they do, of one objective test, two

---

* The analyses in this book of the two sample questions in *Science* first appeared, in substantially the same words, in an article in the October, 1961 issue of *Physics Today,* published by the American Institute of Physics. The reader interested in pursuing the matter further will find additional material in that article and in the February, April, June, and July, 1962 issues of *Physics Today,* and also in the Spring, 1962 issue of *The School Review.*

distinct essay tests, and an oral examination, imply less than overwhelming faith on the part of the psychologists themselves in the efficacy of multiple-choice tests.

But the multiple-choice testers pay little heed to protests. They grow arrogant, claim to be scientific, and use their statistics as a smoke screen. And it is precisely because of this that we have here built a prima facie case against them that rests starkly on the evidence of the challenge questions here presented and the specific defences they elicited. That evidence, I submit, is more than sufficient to justify the setting up of the sort of committee of inquiry that I first proposed in 1959.

The minimum concern of the committee of inquiry would be the quality of multiple-choice tests and their makers. The committee should, of course, have free access to confidential tests whose detailed contents may not be aired in public, and it could hardly avoid discussing the complex question of policing tests to ensure that they meet appropriate standards. For the benefit of defenceless test-takers, it might well formulate a Bill of Rights, among the provisions of which would surely be that difficulty shall not be achieved by means of ambiguity and vagueness. If this provision alone were strictly enforced, it would quickly reveal how limited is the legitimate scope of the multiple-choice test. We have but to recall how ETS, defending the "editor" question, sought to make a virtue out of the presence of ambiguity and subtle distinctions in so-called objective tests.

Only a minority of the committee should consist of professional test-makers and members of the Boards of test-making and test-giving organizations. It should include creative people of commanding intellectual stature who would bring fresh vision to the testing situation, especially as it affects those gifted people whose talents do not conform to the statistically based norms of the multiple-choice testers. Its primary task should be to formulate policy, develop recommendations for remedial action, and propose specific steps to implement its recommendations. In so doing it should consider the whole field of testing in all its aspects, with particular reference to the effects of tests on education, business, and the strength and vitality of the nation—for these are the transcendent issues.

Few people realize how far-reaching are the effects of the current emphasis on multiple-choice tests. These tests have become the dominant factor in educational research; they furnish the yardstick—indeed the very definition—of "progress." When, for example, educators wish to compare the merits of different methods of teaching, they are apt to do so "objectively" and "scientifically" by means of multiple-choice tests, and in the resulting process of natural selection, the "fittest" methods are likely to be those that reflect the shortcomings of the tests.

The wiser testers are well aware of the defects of the multiple-choice format and the danger of placing reliance on any one method of assessment to the exclusion of all others. What is distressing is how little their caveats have impressed the people who succumb to the propaganda of the test-makers and use these tests mechanically as though they were a valid substitute for judgment.

The layman, the business executive, the school administrator, and the indoctrinated teacher, all are apt to be overawed by statistical arguments, and by claims that have the aura if not the substance of science. But the committee of inquiry would be less likely to be impressed by the standard arguments of the multiple-choice test-makers. It would realize not merely that the testers' statistics are less cogent than people are apt to think, but that they are essentially parochial, touching only the immediate and superficial aspects of testing. The committee, with its broad view, would recognize the limitations of these statistics, and would weigh against the statistical case for multiple-choice tests, such as it is, the effect of these tests on education and the nation. It would realize how important it is to train students to organize their own thoughts and to put something of themselves into a project, and how damaging it can be to reward them for merely picking wanted answers at rates up to a hundred an hour. It would realize, as too many testers do not, that the function of tests can not be confined to that of testing. It would be well aware, for example, that though a cure for the common cold might be 99 per cent effective, this admirable statistic, for all its scientific objectivity, would be a dangerously misleading measure of the value of the cure if the cure invariably left the patient crippled; and it would accordingly be far less willing than the testers to sell our intellectual heritage for a mess of statistical pottage.

There is a place for multiple-choice tests, but it is a strictly limited one, and its bounds have long since been overstepped. If a significant proportion of the committee agreed that, except for the most superficial aspects of testing, multiple-choice tests are inherently defective no matter how well they are drafted, that fact alone should be regarded as sufficient reason for seeking to set up an alternative system of testing that would break the tightening stranglehold of the multiple-choice test on our educational system. Admittedly, the widespread use of these tests, to the ever-increasing exclusion of other types of tests, affords a significant economy; but the committee might well wonder whether this was an economy that we, as a nation, can afford.

All methods of evaluating people have their defects—and grave defects they are. But let us not therefore allow one particular method to play the usurper. Let us not seek to replace informed judgment, with all its frailty, by some inexpensive statistical substitute. Let us keep open many diverse and non-competing channels towards recognition. For high ability is where we find it. It is individual and must be recognized for what it is, not rejected out of hand simply because it does not happen to conform to criteria established by statistical technicians. In seeking high ability, let us shun overdependence on tests that are blind to dedication and creativity, and biased against depth and subtlety. For that way lies testolatry.

INDEX

achievement, 20, 101, 106-107, 114
admissions officers, 20, 35, 121, 122, 132
Advanced Placement Program, 114
Aesop, fables, 143
"always," 50-51
ambiguity, 21, 51; and error, 182; intentional, 200-204; objectivity and, 59-76; in science, 182, 183-184
American Association of School Administrators, 111
American Educational Research Association, 101
American Humanist Association, 90
American Institute of Physics, 213*n*
American Scholar, The, 157, 179
Amherst College, 122
answers, the "best," 77-90, 145, 171; court appeal, 62-64; a defense of, 167-171, 175-176, 186-187, 191-195; pedestrian, 101; the right, 80-81, 98; the wanted, 213
aptitude, 101; *see also* Scholastic Aptitude Test
Army Air Force, U.S., 147-148
assumptions, 159-163
Atlantic Monthly, The, 49
"at least," 173-174
atom, light on the, 189-197

Bairnsfather, Bruce, 129
band played on, the, 117-118
Barzun, Jacques, 7-11, 149, 174
Batty, T. C., 17-20
Beethoven, concerto, 22
Beitner, Marvin S., 80-82, 83
Bernstein, Mrs. A., 100
"better 'ole," 129
billiards, 17-21
Binet scale, 145-146
blunders, elementary, 192; unpredictable, 193

bombardiers, 147-148
boomerangs, devising, 155
Bowles, Frank H., 140-141
Brown, Spencer, 119
Buros, Oscar, 38-39, 105
business, the testing, 29-41, 58

calendar, change-over, 27
California Test Bureau, 40
Carroll, John B., 104-106, 138
caveats, 153
Chauncey, Henry, 157, 201, 207
Chicago, University of, 90, 101, 116
Chief State School Officers, Council of, 111
child, a drowsy, 100; the underprivileged, 109-111
City University of New York, 73
Civil Service Commission, New York, 62, 64; U.S., 153-154
cogency, 72
College and University, 140
College Board Review, 113
College Board Scores, 60
college entrance, non-IQ factors, 100-101
College Entrance Examination Board (CEEB), 25-26, 60, 74, 75, 80, 112, 114-117, 138-140, 166-171, 175-181, 205, 206-208; and the atom, 190-191; English composition and, 116-120; influence, 121-122; science explained, 184, 185-188
Commentary, 119
Committee of Examiners in English (CEEB), 207
committee of inquiry, 214
Conant, James B., 105
conundrums, 90
coup de grace, 155
correlations, statistical, 92, 138-140; bias in, 141-142; validity, 56
counselling, 140, 154

A CATALOG OF SELECTED DOVER
BOOKS IN ALL FIELDS OF INTEREST

CONCERNING THE SPIRITUAL IN ART, Wassily Kandinsky. Pioneering work by father of abstract art. Thoughts on color theory, nature of art. Analysis of earlier masters. 12 illustrations. 80pp. of text. 5⅜ x 8½.   23411-8

ANIMALS: 1,419 Copyright-Free Illustrations of Mammals, Birds, Fish, Insects, etc., Jim Harter (ed.). Clear wood engravings present, in extremely lifelike poses, over 1,000 species of animals. One of the most extensive pictorial sourcebooks of its kind. Captions. Index. 284pp. 9 x 12.   23766-4

CELTIC ART: The Methods of Construction, George Bain. Simple geometric techniques for making Celtic interlacements, spirals, Kells-type initials, animals, humans, etc. Over 500 illustrations. 160pp. 9 x 12. (Available in U.S. only.)   22923-8

AN ATLAS OF ANATOMY FOR ARTISTS, Fritz Schider. Most thorough reference work on art anatomy in the world. Hundreds of illustrations, including selections from works by Vesalius, Leonardo, Goya, Ingres, Michelangelo, others. 593 illustrations. 192pp. 7⅛ x 10¼.   20241-0

CELTIC HAND STROKE-BY-STROKE (Irish Half-Uncial from "The Book of Kells"): An Arthur Baker Calligraphy Manual, Arthur Baker. Complete guide to creating each letter of the alphabet in distinctive Celtic manner. Covers hand position, strokes, pens, inks, paper, more. Illustrated. 48pp. 8¼ x 11.   24336-2

EASY ORIGAMI, John Montroll. Charming collection of 32 projects (hat, cup, pelican, piano, swan, many more) specially designed for the novice origami hobbyist. Clearly illustrated easy-to-follow instructions insure that even beginning papercrafters will achieve successful results. 48pp. 8¼ x 11.   27298-2

THE COMPLETE BOOK OF BIRDHOUSE CONSTRUCTION FOR WOOD-WORKERS, Scott D. Campbell. Detailed instructions, illustrations, tables. Also data on bird habitat and instinct patterns. Bibliography. 3 tables. 63 illustrations in 15 figures. 48pp. 5¼ x 8½.   24407-5

BLOOMINGDALE'S ILLUSTRATED 1886 CATALOG: Fashions, Dry Goods and Housewares, Bloomingdale Brothers. Famed merchants' extremely rare catalog depicting about 1,700 products: clothing, housewares, firearms, dry goods, jewelry, more. Invaluable for dating, identifying vintage items. Also, copyright-free graphics for artists, designers. Co-published with Henry Ford Museum & Greenfield Village. 160pp. 8¼ x 11.   25780-0

HISTORIC COSTUME IN PICTURES, Braun & Schneider. Over 1,450 costumed figures in clearly detailed engravings–from dawn of civilization to end of 19th century. Captions. Many folk costumes. 256pp. 8⅜ x 11¾.   23150-X

STICKLEY CRAFTSMAN FURNITURE CATALOGS, Gustav Stickley and L. & J. G. Stickley. Beautiful, functional furniture in two authentic catalogs from 1910. 594 illustrations, including 277 photos, show settles, rockers, armchairs, reclining chairs, bookcases, desks, tables. 183pp. 6½ x 9¼. 23838-5

AMERICAN LOCOMOTIVES IN HISTORIC PHOTOGRAPHS: 1858 to 1949, Ron Ziel (ed.). A rare collection of 126 meticulously detailed official photographs, called "builder portraits," of American locomotives that majestically chronicle the rise of steam locomotive power in America. Introduction. Detailed captions. xi+ 129pp. 9 x 12. 27393-8

AMERICA'S LIGHTHOUSES: An Illustrated History, Francis Ross Holland, Jr. Delightfully written, profusely illustrated fact-filled survey of over 200 American lighthouses since 1716. History, anecdotes, technological advances, more. 240pp. 8 x 10¾. 25576-X

TOWARDS A NEW ARCHITECTURE, Le Corbusier. Pioneering manifesto by founder of "International School." Technical and aesthetic theories, views of industry, economics, relation of form to function, "mass-production split" and much more. Profusely illustrated. 320pp. 6⅛ x 9¼. (Available in U.S. only.) 25023-7

HOW THE OTHER HALF LIVES, Jacob Riis. Famous journalistic record, exposing poverty and degradation of New York slums around 1900, by major social reformer. 100 striking and influential photographs. 233pp. 10 x 7⅞. 22012-5

FRUIT KEY AND TWIG KEY TO TREES AND SHRUBS, William M. Harlow. One of the handiest and most widely used identification aids. Fruit key covers 120 deciduous and evergreen species; twig key 160 deciduous species. Easily used. Over 300 photographs. 126pp. 5⅜ x 8½. 20511-8

COMMON BIRD SONGS, Dr. Donald J. Borror. Songs of 60 most common U.S. birds: robins, sparrows, cardinals, bluejays, finches, more—arranged in order of increasing complexity. Up to 9 variations of songs of each species.
Cassette and manual 99911-4

ORCHIDS AS HOUSE PLANTS, Rebecca Tyson Northen. Grow cattleyas and many other kinds of orchids—in a window, in a case, or under artificial light. 63 illustrations. 148pp. 5⅜ x 8½. 23261-1

MONSTER MAZES, Dave Phillips. Masterful mazes at four levels of difficulty. Avoid deadly perils and evil creatures to find magical treasures. Solutions for all 32 exciting illustrated puzzles. 48pp. 8¼ x 11. 26005-4

MOZART'S DON GIOVANNI (DOVER OPERA LIBRETTO SERIES), Wolfgang Amadeus Mozart. Introduced and translated by Ellen H. Bleiler. Standard Italian libretto, with complete English translation. Convenient and thoroughly portable—an ideal companion for reading along with a recording or the performance itself. Introduction. List of characters. Plot summary. 121pp. 5¼ x 8½. 24944-1

TECHNICAL MANUAL AND DICTIONARY OF CLASSICAL BALLET, Gail Grant. Defines, explains, comments on steps, movements, poses and concepts. 15-page pictorial section. Basic book for student, viewer. 127pp. 5⅜ x 8½. 21843-0

THE CLARINET AND CLARINET PLAYING, David Pino. Lively, comprehensive work features suggestions about technique, musicianship, and musical interpretation, as well as guidelines for teaching, making your own reeds, and preparing for public performance. Includes an intriguing look at clarinet history. "A godsend," *The Clarinet,* Journal of the International Clarinet Society. Appendixes. 7 illus. 320pp. 5⅜ x 8½. 40270-3

HOLLYWOOD GLAMOR PORTRAITS, John Kobal (ed.). 145 photos from 1926-49. Harlow, Gable, Bogart, Bacall; 94 stars in all. Full background on photographers, technical aspects. 160pp. 8⅜ x 11¼. 23352-9

THE ANNOTATED CASEY AT THE BAT: A Collection of Ballads about the Mighty Casey/Third, Revised Edition, Martin Gardner (ed.). Amusing sequels and parodies of one of America's best-loved poems: Casey's Revenge, Why Casey Whiffed, Casey's Sister at the Bat, others. 256pp. 5⅜ x 8½. 28598-7

THE RAVEN AND OTHER FAVORITE POEMS, Edgar Allan Poe. Over 40 of the author's most memorable poems: "The Bells," "Ulalume," "Israfel," "To Helen," "The Conqueror Worm," "Eldorado," "Annabel Lee," many more. Alphabetic lists of titles and first lines. 64pp. 5³⁄₁₆ x 8¼. 26685-0

PERSONAL MEMOIRS OF U. S. GRANT, Ulysses Simpson Grant. Intelligent, deeply moving firsthand account of Civil War campaigns, considered by many the finest military memoirs ever written. Includes letters, historic photographs, maps and more. 528pp. 6⅛ x 9¼. 28587-1

ANCIENT EGYPTIAN MATERIALS AND INDUSTRIES, A. Lucas and J. Harris. Fascinating, comprehensive, thoroughly documented text describes this ancient civilization's vast resources and the processes that incorporated them in daily life, including the use of animal products, building materials, cosmetics, perfumes and incense, fibers, glazed ware, glass and its manufacture, materials used in the mummification process, and much more. 544pp. 6¹⁄₈ x 9¹⁄₄. (Available in U.S. only.) 40446-3

RUSSIAN STORIES/RUSSKIE RASSKAZY: A Dual-Language Book, edited by Gleb Struve. Twelve tales by such masters as Chekhov, Tolstoy, Dostoevsky, Pushkin, others. Excellent word-for-word English translations on facing pages, plus teaching and study aids, Russian/English vocabulary, biographical/critical introductions, more. 416pp. 5⅜ x 8½. 26244-8

PHILADELPHIA THEN AND NOW: 60 Sites Photographed in the Past and Present, Kenneth Finkel and Susan Oyama. Rare photographs of City Hall, Logan Square, Independence Hall, Betsy Ross House, other landmarks juxtaposed with contemporary views. Captures changing face of historic city. Introduction. Captions. 128pp. 8¼ x 11. 25790-8

AIA ARCHITECTURAL GUIDE TO NASSAU AND SUFFOLK COUNTIES, LONG ISLAND, The American Institute of Architects, Long Island Chapter, and the Society for the Preservation of Long Island Antiquities. Comprehensive, well-researched and generously illustrated volume brings to life over three centuries of Long Island's great architectural heritage. More than 240 photographs with authoritative, extensively detailed captions. 176pp. 8¼ x 11. 26946-9

NORTH AMERICAN INDIAN LIFE: Customs and Traditions of 23 Tribes, Elsie Clews Parsons (ed.). 27 fictionalized essays by noted anthropologists examine religion, customs, government, additional facets of life among the Winnebago, Crow, Zuni, Eskimo, other tribes. 480pp. 6⅛ x 9¼. 27377-6

FRANK LLOYD WRIGHT'S DANA HOUSE, Donald Hoffmann. Pictorial essay of residential masterpiece with over 160 interior and exterior photos, plans, elevations, sketches and studies. 128pp. 9¼ x 10¾.　　29120-0

THE MALE AND FEMALE FIGURE IN MOTION: 60 Classic Photographic Sequences, Eadweard Muybridge. 60 true-action photographs of men and women walking, running, climbing, bending, turning, etc., reproduced from rare 19th-century masterpiece. vi + 121pp. 9 x 12.　　24745-7

1001 QUESTIONS ANSWERED ABOUT THE SEASHORE, N. J. Berrill and Jacquelyn Berrill. Queries answered about dolphins, sea snails, sponges, starfish, fishes, shore birds, many others. Covers appearance, breeding, growth, feeding, much more. 305pp. 5¼ x 8¼.　　23366-9

ATTRACTING BIRDS TO YOUR YARD, William J. Weber. Easy-to-follow guide offers advice on how to attract the greatest diversity of birds: birdhouses, feeders, water and waterers, much more. 96pp. 5³⁄₁₆ x 8¼.　　28927-3

MEDICINAL AND OTHER USES OF NORTH AMERICAN PLANTS: A Historical Survey with Special Reference to the Eastern Indian Tribes, Charlotte Erichsen-Brown. Chronological historical citations document 500 years of usage of plants, trees, shrubs native to eastern Canada, northeastern U.S. Also complete identifying information. 343 illustrations. 544pp. 6½ x 9¼.　　25951-X

STORYBOOK MAZES, Dave Phillips. 23 stories and mazes on two-page spreads: Wizard of Oz, Treasure Island, Robin Hood, etc. Solutions. 64pp. 8¼ x 11.　23628-5

AMERICAN NEGRO SONGS: 230 Folk Songs and Spirituals, Religious and Secular, John W. Work. This authoritative study traces the African influences of songs sung and played by black Americans at work, in church, and as entertainment. The author discusses the lyric significance of such songs as "Swing Low, Sweet Chariot," "John Henry," and others and offers the words and music for 230 songs. Bibliography. Index of Song Titles. 272pp. 6½ x 9¼.　　40271-1

MOVIE-STAR PORTRAITS OF THE FORTIES, John Kobal (ed.). 163 glamor, studio photos of 106 stars of the 1940s: Rita Hayworth, Ava Gardner, Marlon Brando, Clark Gable, many more. 176pp. 8⅜ x 11¼.　　23546-7

BENCHLEY LOST AND FOUND, Robert Benchley. Finest humor from early 30s, about pet peeves, child psychologists, post office and others. Mostly unavailable elsewhere. 73 illustrations by Peter Arno and others. 183pp. 5⅜ x 8½.　　22410-4

YEKL and THE IMPORTED BRIDEGROOM AND OTHER STORIES OF YIDDISH NEW YORK, Abraham Cahan. Film Hester Street based on *Yekl* (1896). Novel, other stories among first about Jewish immigrants on N.Y.'s East Side. 240pp. 5⅜ x 8½.　　22427-9

SELECTED POEMS, Walt Whitman. Generous sampling from *Leaves of Grass*. Twenty-four poems include "I Hear America Singing," "Song of the Open Road," "I Sing the Body Electric," "When Lilacs Last in the Dooryard Bloom'd," "O Captain! My Captain!"—all reprinted from an authoritative edition. Lists of titles and first lines. 128pp. 5³⁄₁₆ x 8¼.　　26878-0

THE BEST TALES OF HOFFMANN, E. T. A. Hoffmann. 10 of Hoffmann's most important stories: "Nutcracker and the King of Mice," "The Golden Flowerpot," etc. 458pp. 5⅜ x 8½.   21793-0

FROM FETISH TO GOD IN ANCIENT EGYPT, E. A. Wallis Budge. Rich detailed survey of Egyptian conception of "God" and gods, magic, cult of animals, Osiris, more. Also, superb English translations of hymns and legends. 240 illustrations. 545pp. 5⅜ x 8½.   25803-3

FRENCH STORIES/CONTES FRANÇAIS: A Dual-Language Book, Wallace Fowlie. Ten stories by French masters, Voltaire to Camus: "Micromegas" by Voltaire; "The Atheist's Mass" by Balzac; "Minuet" by de Maupassant; "The Guest" by Camus, six more. Excellent English translations on facing pages. Also French-English vocabulary list, exercises, more. 352pp. 5⅜ x 8½.   26443-2

CHICAGO AT THE TURN OF THE CENTURY IN PHOTOGRAPHS: 122 Historic Views from the Collections of the Chicago Historical Society, Larry A. Viskochil. Rare large-format prints offer detailed views of City Hall, State Street, the Loop, Hull House, Union Station, many other landmarks, circa 1904-1913. Introduction. Captions. Maps. 144pp. 9⅜ x 12¼.   24656-6

OLD BROOKLYN IN EARLY PHOTOGRAPHS, 1865-1929, William Lee Younger. Luna Park, Gravesend race track, construction of Grand Army Plaza, moving of Hotel Brighton, etc. 157 previously unpublished photographs. 165pp. 8⅞ x 11¾.
                                                                        23587-4

THE MYTHS OF THE NORTH AMERICAN INDIANS, Lewis Spence. Rich anthology of the myths and legends of the Algonquins, Iroquois, Pawnees and Sioux, prefaced by an extensive historical and ethnological commentary. 36 illustrations. 480pp. 5⅜ x 8½.   25967-6

AN ENCYCLOPEDIA OF BATTLES: Accounts of Over 1,560 Battles from 1479 B.C. to the Present, David Eggenberger. Essential details of every major battle in recorded history from the first battle of Megiddo in 1479 B.C. to Grenada in 1984. List of Battle Maps. New Appendix covering the years 1967-1984. Index. 99 illustrations. 544pp. 6½ x 9¼.   24913-1

SAILING ALONE AROUND THE WORLD, Captain Joshua Slocum. First man to sail around the world, alone, in small boat. One of great feats of seamanship told in delightful manner. 67 illustrations. 294pp. 5⅜ x 8½.   20326-3

ANARCHISM AND OTHER ESSAYS, Emma Goldman. Powerful, penetrating, prophetic essays on direct action, role of minorities, prison reform, puritan hypocrisy, violence, etc. 271pp. 5⅜ x 8½.   22484-8

MYTHS OF THE HINDUS AND BUDDHISTS, Ananda K. Coomaraswamy and Sister Nivedita. Great stories of the epics; deeds of Krishna, Shiva, taken from puranas, Vedas, folk tales; etc. 32 illustrations. 400pp. 5⅜ x 8½.   21759-0

THE TRAUMA OF BIRTH, Otto Rank. Rank's controversial thesis that anxiety neurosis is caused by profound psychological trauma which occurs at birth. 256pp. 5⅜ x 8½.   27974-X

A THEOLOGICO-POLITICAL TREATISE, Benedict Spinoza. Also contains unfinished Political Treatise. Great classic on religious liberty, theory of government on common consent. R. Elwes translation. Total of 421pp. 5⅜ x 8½.   20249-6

CATALOG OF DOVER BOOKS

MY BONDAGE AND MY FREEDOM, Frederick Douglass. Born a slave, Douglass became outspoken force in antislavery movement. The best of Douglass' autobiographies. Graphic description of slave life. 464pp. 5⅜ x 8½. 22457-0

FOLLOWING THE EQUATOR: A Journey Around the World, Mark Twain. Fascinating humorous account of 1897 voyage to Hawaii, Australia, India, New Zealand, etc. Ironic, bemused reports on peoples, customs, climate, flora and fauna, politics, much more. 197 illustrations. 720pp. 5⅜ x 8½. 26113-1

THE PEOPLE CALLED SHAKERS, Edward D. Andrews. Definitive study of Shakers: origins, beliefs, practices, dances, social organization, furniture and crafts, etc. 33 illustrations. 351pp. 5⅜ x 8½. 21081-2

THE MYTHS OF GREECE AND ROME, H. A. Guerber. A classic of mythology, generously illustrated, long prized for its simple, graphic, accurate retelling of the principal myths of Greece and Rome, and for its commentary on their origins and significance. With 64 illustrations by Michelangelo, Raphael, Titian, Rubens, Canova, Bernini and others. 480pp. 5⅜ x 8½. 27584-1

PSYCHOLOGY OF MUSIC, Carl E. Seashore. Classic work discusses music as a medium from psychological viewpoint. Clear treatment of physical acoustics, auditory apparatus, sound perception, development of musical skills, nature of musical feeling, host of other topics. 88 figures. 408pp. 5⅜ x 8½. 21851-1

THE PHILOSOPHY OF HISTORY, Georg W. Hegel. Great classic of Western thought develops concept that history is not chance but rational process, the evolution of freedom. 457pp. 5⅜ x 8½. 20112-0

THE BOOK OF TEA, Kakuzo Okakura. Minor classic of the Orient: entertaining, charming explanation, interpretation of traditional Japanese culture in terms of tea ceremony. 94pp. 5⅜ x 8½. 20070-1

LIFE IN ANCIENT EGYPT, Adolf Erman. Fullest, most thorough, detailed older account with much not in more recent books, domestic life, religion, magic, medicine, commerce, much more. Many illustrations reproduce tomb paintings, carvings, hieroglyphs, etc. 597pp. 5⅜ x 8½. 22632-8

SUNDIALS, Their Theory and Construction, Albert Waugh. Far and away the best, most thorough coverage of ideas, mathematics concerned, types, construction, adjusting anywhere. Simple, nontechnical treatment allows even children to build several of these dials. Over 100 illustrations. 230pp. 5⅜ x 8½. 22947-5

THEORETICAL HYDRODYNAMICS, L. M. Milne-Thomson. Classic exposition of the mathematical theory of fluid motion, applicable to both hydrodynamics and aerodynamics. Over 600 exercises. 768pp. 6⅛ x 9¼. 68970-0

SONGS OF EXPERIENCE: Facsimile Reproduction with 26 Plates in Full Color, William Blake. 26 full-color plates from a rare 1826 edition. Includes "The Tyger," "London," "Holy Thursday," and other poems. Printed text of poems. 48pp. 5¼ x 7. 24636-1

OLD-TIME VIGNETTES IN FULL COLOR, Carol Belanger Grafton (ed.). Over 390 charming, often sentimental illustrations, selected from archives of Victorian graphics–pretty women posing, children playing, food, flowers, kittens and puppies, smiling cherubs, birds and butterflies, much more. All copyright-free. 48pp. 9¼ x 12¼. 27269-9

PERSPECTIVE FOR ARTISTS, Rex Vicat Cole. Depth, perspective of sky and sea, shadows, much more, not usually covered. 391 diagrams, 81 reproductions of drawings and paintings. 279pp. 5⅜ x 8½. 22487-2

DRAWING THE LIVING FIGURE, Joseph Sheppard. Innovative approach to artistic anatomy focuses on specifics of surface anatomy, rather than muscles and bones. Over 170 drawings of live models in front, back and side views, and in widely varying poses. Accompanying diagrams. 177 illustrations. Introduction. Index. 144pp. 8⅜ x11¼. 26723-7

GOTHIC AND OLD ENGLISH ALPHABETS: 100 Complete Fonts, Dan X. Solo. Add power, elegance to posters, signs, other graphics with 100 stunning copyright-free alphabets: Blackstone, Dolbey, Germania, 97 more–including many lower-case, numerals, punctuation marks. 104pp. 8⅛ x 11. 24695-7

HOW TO DO BEADWORK, Mary White. Fundamental book on craft from simple projects to five-bead chains and woven works. 106 illustrations. 142pp. 5⅜ x 8. 20697-1

THE BOOK OF WOOD CARVING, Charles Marshall Sayers. Finest book for beginners discusses fundamentals and offers 34 designs. "Absolutely first rate . . . well thought out and well executed."–E. J. Tangerman. 118pp. 7¾ x 10⅝. 23654-4

ILLUSTRATED CATALOG OF CIVIL WAR MILITARY GOODS: Union Army Weapons, Insignia, Uniform Accessories, and Other Equipment, Schuyler, Hartley, and Graham. Rare, profusely illustrated 1846 catalog includes Union Army uniform and dress regulations, arms and ammunition, coats, insignia, flags, swords, rifles, etc. 226 illustrations. 160pp. 9 x 12. 24939-5

WOMEN'S FASHIONS OF THE EARLY 1900s: An Unabridged Republication of "New York Fashions, 1909," National Cloak & Suit Co. Rare catalog of mail-order fashions documents women's and children's clothing styles shortly after the turn of the century. Captions offer full descriptions, prices. Invaluable resource for fashion, costume historians. Approximately 725 illustrations. 128pp. 8⅜ x 11¼. 27276-1

THE 1912 AND 1915 GUSTAV STICKLEY FURNITURE CATALOGS, Gustav Stickley. With over 200 detailed illustrations and descriptions, these two catalogs are essential reading and reference materials and identification guides for Stickley furniture. Captions cite materials, dimensions and prices. 112pp. 6½ x 9¼. 26676-1

EARLY AMERICAN LOCOMOTIVES, John H. White, Jr. Finest locomotive engravings from early 19th century: historical (1804–74), main-line (after 1870), special, foreign, etc. 147 plates. 142pp. 11⅜ x 8¼. 22772-3

THE TALL SHIPS OF TODAY IN PHOTOGRAPHS, Frank O. Braynard. Lavishly illustrated tribute to nearly 100 majestic contemporary sailing vessels: Amerigo Vespucci, Clearwater, Constitution, Eagle, Mayflower, Sea Cloud, Victory, many more. Authoritative captions provide statistics, background on each ship. 190 black-and-white photographs and illustrations. Introduction. 128pp. 8⅞ x 11¾. 27163-3

LITTLE BOOK OF EARLY AMERICAN CRAFTS AND TRADES, Peter Stockham (ed.). 1807 children's book explains crafts and trades: baker, hatter, cooper, potter, and many others. 23 copperplate illustrations. 140pp. 4⅝ x 6. 23336-7

VICTORIAN FASHIONS AND COSTUMES FROM HARPER'S BAZAR, 1867–1898, Stella Blum (ed.). Day costumes, evening wear, sports clothes, shoes, hats, other accessories in over 1,000 detailed engravings. 320pp. 9⅜ x 12¼. 22990-4

GUSTAV STICKLEY, THE CRAFTSMAN, Mary Ann Smith. Superb study surveys broad scope of Stickley's achievement, especially in architecture. Design philosophy, rise and fall of the Craftsman empire, descriptions and floor plans for many Craftsman houses, more. 86 black-and-white halftones. 31 line illustrations. Introduction 208pp. 6½ x 9¼. 27210-9

THE LONG ISLAND RAIL ROAD IN EARLY PHOTOGRAPHS, Ron Ziel. Over 220 rare photos, informative text document origin (1844) and development of rail service on Long Island. Vintage views of early trains, locomotives, stations, passengers, crews, much more. Captions. 8⅞ x 11¾. 26301-0

VOYAGE OF THE LIBERDADE, Joshua Slocum. Great 19th-century mariner's thrilling, first-hand account of the wreck of his ship off South America, the 35-foot boat he built from the wreckage, and its remarkable voyage home. 128pp. 5⅜ x 8½. 40022-0

TEN BOOKS ON ARCHITECTURE, Vitruvius. The most important book ever written on architecture. Early Roman aesthetics, technology, classical orders, site selection, all other aspects. Morgan translation. 331pp. 5⅜ x 8½. 20645-9

THE HUMAN FIGURE IN MOTION, Eadweard Muybridge. More than 4,500 stopped-action photos, in action series, showing undraped men, women, children jumping, lying down, throwing, sitting, wrestling, carrying, etc. 390pp. 7⅞ x 10⅝. 20204-6 Clothbd.

TREES OF THE EASTERN AND CENTRAL UNITED STATES AND CANADA, William M. Harlow. Best one-volume guide to 140 trees. Full descriptions, woodlore, range, etc. Over 600 illustrations. Handy size. 288pp. 4½ x 6⅜. 20395-6

SONGS OF WESTERN BIRDS, Dr. Donald J. Borror. Complete song and call repertoire of 60 western species, including flycatchers, juncoes, cactus wrens, many more–includes fully illustrated booklet. Cassette and manual 99913-0

GROWING AND USING HERBS AND SPICES, Milo Miloradovich. Versatile handbook provides all the information needed for cultivation and use of all the herbs and spices available in North America. 4 illustrations. Index. Glossary. 236pp. 5⅜ x 8½. 25058-X

BIG BOOK OF MAZES AND LABYRINTHS, Walter Shepherd. 50 mazes and labyrinths in all–classical, solid, ripple, and more–in one great volume. Perfect inexpensive puzzler for clever youngsters. Full solutions. 112pp. 8⅛ x 11. 22951-3

PIANO TUNING, J. Cree Fischer. Clearest, best book for beginner, amateur. Simple repairs, raising dropped notes, tuning by easy method of flattened fifths. No previous skills needed. 4 illustrations. 201pp. 5⅜ x 8½. 23267-0

HINTS TO SINGERS, Lillian Nordica. Selecting the right teacher, developing confidence, overcoming stage fright, and many other important skills receive thoughtful discussion in this indispensible guide, written by a world-famous diva of four decades' experience. 96pp. 5⅜ x 8½. 40094-8

THE COMPLETE NONSENSE OF EDWARD LEAR, Edward Lear. All nonsense limericks, zany alphabets, Owl and Pussycat, songs, nonsense botany, etc., illustrated by Lear. Total of 320pp. 5⅜ x 8½. (Available in U.S. only.) 20167-8

VICTORIAN PARLOUR POETRY: An Annotated Anthology, Michael R. Turner. 117 gems by Longfellow, Tennyson, Browning, many lesser-known poets. "The Village Blacksmith," "Curfew Must Not Ring Tonight," "Only a Baby Small," dozens more, often difficult to find elsewhere. Index of poets, titles, first lines. xxiii + 325pp. 5⅝ x 8¼. 27044-0

DUBLINERS, James Joyce. Fifteen stories offer vivid, tightly focused observations of the lives of Dublin's poorer classes. At least one, "The Dead," is considered a masterpiece. Reprinted complete and unabridged from standard edition. 160pp. 5³⁄₁₆ x 8¼. 26870-5

GREAT WEIRD TALES: 14 Stories by Lovecraft, Blackwood, Machen and Others, S. T. Joshi (ed.). 14 spellbinding tales, including "The Sin Eater," by Fiona McLeod, "The Eye Above the Mantel," by Frank Belknap Long, as well as renowned works by R. H. Barlow, Lord Dunsany, Arthur Machen, W. C. Morrow and eight other masters of the genre. 256pp. 5⅜ x 8½. (Available in U.S. only.) 40436-6

THE BOOK OF THE SACRED MAGIC OF ABRAMELIN THE MAGE, translated by S. MacGregor Mathers. Medieval manuscript of ceremonial magic. Basic document in Aleister Crowley, Golden Dawn groups. 268pp. 5⅜ x 8½. 23211-5

NEW RUSSIAN-ENGLISH AND ENGLISH-RUSSIAN DICTIONARY, M. A. O'Brien. This is a remarkably handy Russian dictionary, containing a surprising amount of information, including over 70,000 entries. 366pp. 4½ x 6⅛. 20208-9

HISTORIC HOMES OF THE AMERICAN PRESIDENTS, Second, Revised Edition, Irvin Haas. A traveler's guide to American Presidential homes, most open to the public, depicting and describing homes occupied by every American President from George Washington to George Bush. With visiting hours, admission charges, travel routes. 175 photographs. Index. 160pp. 8¼ x 11. 26751-2

NEW YORK IN THE FORTIES, Andreas Feininger. 162 brilliant photographs by the well-known photographer, formerly with *Life* magazine. Commuters, shoppers, Times Square at night, much else from city at its peak. Captions by John von Hartz. 181pp. 9¼ x 10¾. 23585-8

INDIAN SIGN LANGUAGE, William Tomkins. Over 525 signs developed by Sioux and other tribes. Written instructions and diagrams. Also 290 pictographs. 111pp. 6⅛ x 9¼. 22029-X

ANATOMY: A Complete Guide for Artists, Joseph Sheppard. A master of figure drawing shows artists how to render human anatomy convincingly. Over 460 illustrations. 224pp. 8⅜ x 11¼. 27279-6

MEDIEVAL CALLIGRAPHY: Its History and Technique, Marc Drogin. Spirited history, comprehensive instruction manual covers 13 styles (ca. 4th century through 15th). Excellent photographs; directions for duplicating medieval techniques with modern tools. 224pp. 8⅜ x 11¼. 26142-5

DRIED FLOWERS: How to Prepare Them, Sarah Whitlock and Martha Rankin. Complete instructions on how to use silica gel, meal and borax, perlite aggregate, sand and borax, glycerine and water to create attractive permanent flower arrangements. 12 illustrations. 32pp. 5⅜ x 8½. 21802-3

EASY-TO-MAKE BIRD FEEDERS FOR WOODWORKERS, Scott D. Campbell. Detailed, simple-to-use guide for designing, constructing, caring for and using feeders. Text, illustrations for 12 classic and contemporary designs. 96pp. 5⅜ x 8½. 25847-5

SCOTTISH WONDER TALES FROM MYTH AND LEGEND, Donald A. Mackenzie. 16 lively tales tell of giants rumbling down mountainsides, of a magic wand that turns stone pillars into warriors, of gods and goddesses, evil hags, powerful forces and more. 240pp. 5⅜ x 8½. 29677-6

THE HISTORY OF UNDERCLOTHES, C. Willett Cunnington and Phyllis Cunnington. Fascinating, well-documented survey covering six centuries of English undergarments, enhanced with over 100 illustrations: 12th-century laced-up bodice, footed long drawers (1795), 19th-century bustles, l9th-century corsets for men, Victorian "bust improvers," much more. 272pp. 5⅜ x 8¼. 27124-2

ARTS AND CRAFTS FURNITURE: The Complete Brooks Catalog of 1912, Brooks Manufacturing Co. Photos and detailed descriptions of more than 150 now very collectible furniture designs from the Arts and Crafts movement depict davenports, settees, buffets, desks, tables, chairs, bedsteads, dressers and more, all built of solid, quarter-sawed oak. Invaluable for students and enthusiasts of antiques, Americana and the decorative arts. 80pp. 6½ x 9¼. 27471-3

WILBUR AND ORVILLE: A Biography of the Wright Brothers, Fred Howard. Definitive, crisply written study tells the full story of the brothers' lives and work. A vividly written biography, unparalleled in scope and color, that also captures the spirit of an extraordinary era. 560pp. 6⅛ x 9¼. 40297-5

THE ARTS OF THE SAILOR: Knotting, Splicing and Ropework, Hervey Garrett Smith. Indispensable shipboard reference covers tools, basic knots and useful hitches; handsewing and canvas work, more. Over 100 illustrations. Delightful reading for sea lovers. 256pp. 5⅜ x 8½. 26440-8

FRANK LLOYD WRIGHT'S FALLINGWATER: The House and Its History, Second, Revised Edition, Donald Hoffmann. A total revision—both in text and illustrations—of the standard document on Fallingwater, the boldest, most personal architectural statement of Wright's mature years, updated with valuable new material from the recently opened Frank Lloyd Wright Archives. "Fascinating"–*The New York Times*. 116 illustrations. 128pp. 9¼ x 10¾. 27430-6

PHOTOGRAPHIC SKETCHBOOK OF THE CIVIL WAR, Alexander Gardner. 100 photos taken on field during the Civil War. Famous shots of Manassas Harper's Ferry, Lincoln, Richmond, slave pens, etc. 244pp. 10⅝ x 8¼. 22731-6

FIVE ACRES AND INDEPENDENCE, Maurice G. Kains. Great back-to-the-land classic explains basics of self-sufficient farming. The one book to get. 95 illustrations. 397pp. 5⅜ x 8½. 20974-1

SONGS OF EASTERN BIRDS, Dr. Donald J. Borror. Songs and calls of 60 species most common to eastern U.S.: warblers, woodpeckers, flycatchers, thrushes, larks, many more in high-quality recording. Cassette and manual 99912-2

A MODERN HERBAL, Margaret Grieve. Much the fullest, most exact, most useful compilation of herbal material. Gigantic alphabetical encyclopedia, from aconite to zedoary, gives botanical information, medical properties, folklore, economic uses, much else. Indispensable to serious reader. 161 illustrations. 888pp. 6½ x 9¼. 2-vol. set. (Available in U.S. only.) Vol. I: 22798-7
Vol. II: 22799-5

HIDDEN TREASURE MAZE BOOK, Dave Phillips. Solve 34 challenging mazes accompanied by heroic tales of adventure. Evil dragons, people-eating plants, blood-thirsty giants, many more dangerous adversaries lurk at every twist and turn. 34 mazes, stories, solutions. 48pp. 8¼ x 11. 24566-7

LETTERS OF W. A. MOZART, Wolfgang A. Mozart. Remarkable letters show bawdy wit, humor, imagination, musical insights, contemporary musical world; includes some letters from Leopold Mozart. 276pp. 5⅜ x 8½. 22859-2

BASIC PRINCIPLES OF CLASSICAL BALLET, Agrippina Vaganova. Great Russian theoretician, teacher explains methods for teaching classical ballet. 118 illustrations. 175pp. 5⅜ x 8½. 22036-2

THE JUMPING FROG, Mark Twain. Revenge edition. The original story of The Celebrated Jumping Frog of Calaveras County, a hapless French translation, and Twain's hilarious "retranslation" from the French. 12 illustrations. 66pp. 5⅜ x 8½. 22686-7

BEST REMEMBERED POEMS, Martin Gardner (ed.). The 126 poems in this superb collection of 19th- and 20th-century British and American verse range from Shelley's "To a Skylark" to the impassioned "Renascence" of Edna St. Vincent Millay and to Edward Lear's whimsical "The Owl and the Pussycat." 224pp. 5⅜ x 8½. 27165-X

COMPLETE SONNETS, William Shakespeare. Over 150 exquisite poems deal with love, friendship, the tyranny of time, beauty's evanescence, death and other themes in language of remarkable power, precision and beauty. Glossary of archaic terms. 80pp. 5³⁄₁₆ x 8¼. 26686-9

THE BATTLES THAT CHANGED HISTORY, Fletcher Pratt. Eminent historian profiles 16 crucial conflicts, ancient to modern, that changed the course of civilization. 352pp. 5⅜ x 8½. 41129-X

THE WIT AND HUMOR OF OSCAR WILDE, Alvin Redman (ed.). More than 1,000 ripostes, paradoxes, wisecracks: Work is the curse of the drinking classes; I can resist everything except temptation; etc. 258pp. 5⅜ x 8½. 20602-5

SHAKESPEARE LEXICON AND QUOTATION DICTIONARY, Alexander Schmidt. Full definitions, locations, shades of meaning in every word in plays and poems. More than 50,000 exact quotations. 1,485pp. 6½ x 9¼. 2-vol. set.
Vol. 1: 22726-X
Vol. 2: 22727-8

SELECTED POEMS, Emily Dickinson. Over 100 best-known, best-loved poems by one of America's foremost poets, reprinted from authoritative early editions. No comparable edition at this price. Index of first lines. 64pp. 5³⁄₁₆ x 8¼. 26466-1

THE INSIDIOUS DR. FU-MANCHU, Sax Rohmer. The first of the popular mystery series introduces a pair of English detectives to their archnemesis, the diabolical Dr. Fu-Manchu. Flavorful atmosphere, fast-paced action, and colorful characters enliven this classic of the genre. 208pp. 5³⁄₁₆ x 8¼. 29898-1

THE MALLEUS MALEFICARUM OF KRAMER AND SPRENGER, translated by Montague Summers. Full text of most important witchhunter's "bible," used by both Catholics and Protestants. 278pp. 6⅝ x 10. 22802-9

SPANISH STORIES/CUENTOS ESPAÑOLES: A Dual-Language Book, Angel Flores (ed.). Unique format offers 13 great stories in Spanish by Cervantes, Borges, others. Faithful English translations on facing pages. 352pp. 5⅜ x 8½. 25399-6

GARDEN CITY, LONG ISLAND, IN EARLY PHOTOGRAPHS, 1869–1919, Mildred H. Smith. Handsome treasury of 118 vintage pictures, accompanied by carefully researched captions, document the Garden City Hotel fire (1899), the Vanderbilt Cup Race (1908), the first airmail flight departing from the Nassau Boulevard Aerodrome (1911), and much more. 96pp. 8⅞ x 11¾. 40669-5

OLD QUEENS, N.Y., IN EARLY PHOTOGRAPHS, Vincent F. Seyfried and William Asadorian. Over 160 rare photographs of Maspeth, Jamaica, Jackson Heights, and other areas. Vintage views of DeWitt Clinton mansion, 1939 World's Fair and more. Captions. 192pp. 8⅞ x 11. 26358-4

CAPTURED BY THE INDIANS: 15 Firsthand Accounts, 1750-1870, Frederick Drimmer. Astounding true historical accounts of grisly torture, bloody conflicts, relentless pursuits, miraculous escapes and more, by people who lived to tell the tale. 384pp. 5⅜ x 8½. 24901-8

THE WORLD'S GREAT SPEECHES (Fourth Enlarged Edition), Lewis Copeland, Lawrence W. Lamm, and Stephen J. McKenna. Nearly 300 speeches provide public speakers with a wealth of updated quotes and inspiration–from Pericles' funeral oration and William Jennings Bryan's "Cross of Gold Speech" to Malcolm X's powerful words on the Black Revolution and Earl of Spenser's tribute to his sister, Diana, Princess of Wales. 944pp. 5⅜ x 8⅜. 40903-1

THE BOOK OF THE SWORD, Sir Richard F. Burton. Great Victorian scholar/adventurer's eloquent, erudite history of the "queen of weapons"–from prehistory to early Roman Empire. Evolution and development of early swords, variations (sabre, broadsword, cutlass, scimitar, etc.), much more. 336pp. 6⅛ x 9¼. 25434-8

AUTOBIOGRAPHY: The Story of My Experiments with Truth, Mohandas K. Gandhi. Boyhood, legal studies, purification, the growth of the Satyagraha (nonviolent protest) movement. Critical, inspiring work of the man responsible for the freedom of India. 480pp. 5⅜ x 8½. (Available in U.S. only.) 24593-4

CELTIC MYTHS AND LEGENDS, T. W. Rolleston. Masterful retelling of Irish and Welsh stories and tales. Cuchulain, King Arthur, Deirdre, the Grail, many more. First paperback edition. 58 full-page illustrations. 512pp. 5⅜ x 8½. 26507-2

THE PRINCIPLES OF PSYCHOLOGY, William James. Famous long course complete, unabridged. Stream of thought, time perception, memory, experimental methods; great work decades ahead of its time. 94 figures. 1,391pp. 5⅜ x 8½. 2-vol. set. Vol. I: 20381-6 Vol. II: 20382-4

THE WORLD AS WILL AND REPRESENTATION, Arthur Schopenhauer. Definitive English translation of Schopenhauer's life work, correcting more than 1,000 errors, omissions in earlier translations. Translated by E. F. J. Payne. Total of 1,269pp. 5⅜ x 8½. 2-vol. set. Vol. 1: 21761-2 Vol. 2: 21762-0

MAGIC AND MYSTERY IN TIBET, Madame Alexandra David-Neel. Experiences among lamas, magicians, sages, sorcerers, Bonpa wizards. A true psychic discovery. 32 illustrations. 321pp. 5⅜ x 8½. (Available in U.S. only.) 22682-4

THE EGYPTIAN BOOK OF THE DEAD, E. A. Wallis Budge. Complete reproduction of Ani's papyrus, finest ever found. Full hieroglyphic text, interlinear transliteration, word-for-word translation, smooth translation. 533pp. 6½ x 9¼. 21866-X

MATHEMATICS FOR THE NONMATHEMATICIAN, Morris Kline. Detailed, college-level treatment of mathematics in cultural and historical context, with numerous exercises. Recommended Reading Lists. Tables. Numerous figures. 641pp. 5⅜ x 8½. 24823-2

PROBABILISTIC METHODS IN THE THEORY OF STRUCTURES, Isaac Elishakoff. Well-written introduction covers the elements of the theory of probability from two or more random variables, the reliability of such multivariable structures, the theory of random function, Monte Carlo methods of treating problems incapable of exact solution, and more. Examples. 502pp. 5⅜ x 8½. 40691-1

THE RIME OF THE ANCIENT MARINER, Gustave Doré, S. T. Coleridge. Doré's finest work; 34 plates capture moods, subtleties of poem. Flawless full-size reproductions printed on facing pages with authoritative text of poem. "Beautiful. Simply beautiful."–*Publisher's Weekly*. 77pp. 9¼ x 12. 22305-1

NORTH AMERICAN INDIAN DESIGNS FOR ARTISTS AND CRAFTSPEOPLE, Eva Wilson. Over 360 authentic copyright-free designs adapted from Navajo blankets, Hopi pottery, Sioux buffalo hides, more. Geometrics, symbolic figures, plant and animal motifs, etc. 128pp. 8⅜ x 11. (Not for sale in the United Kingdom.) 25341-4

SCULPTURE: Principles and Practice, Louis Slobodkin. Step-by-step approach to clay, plaster, metals, stone; classical and modern. 253 drawings, photos. 255pp. 8⅛ x 11. 22960-2

THE INFLUENCE OF SEA POWER UPON HISTORY, 1660–1783, A. T. Mahan. Influential classic of naval history and tactics still used as text in war colleges. First paperback edition. 4 maps. 24 battle plans. 640pp. 5⅜ x 8½. 25509-3

THE STORY OF THE TITANIC AS TOLD BY ITS SURVIVORS, Jack Winocour (ed.). What it was really like. Panic, despair, shocking inefficiency, and a little heroism. More thrilling than any fictional account. 26 illustrations. 320pp. 5⅜ x 8½.
20610-6

FAIRY AND FOLK TALES OF THE IRISH PEASANTRY, William Butler Yeats (ed.). Treasury of 64 tales from the twilight world of Celtic myth and legend: "The Soul Cages," "The Kildare Pooka," "King O'Toole and his Goose," many more. Introduction and Notes by W. B. Yeats. 352pp. 5⅜ x 8½. 26941-8

BUDDHIST MAHAYANA TEXTS, E. B. Cowell and others (eds.). Superb, accurate translations of basic documents in Mahayana Buddhism, highly important in history of religions. The Buddha-karita of Asvaghosha, Larger Sukhavativyuha, more. 448pp. 5⅜ x 8½. 25552-2

ONE TWO THREE . . . INFINITY: Facts and Speculations of Science, George Gamow. Great physicist's fascinating, readable overview of contemporary science: number theory, relativity, fourth dimension, entropy, genes, atomic structure, much more. 128 illustrations. Index. 352pp. 5⅜ x 8½. 25664-2

EXPERIMENTATION AND MEASUREMENT, W. J. Youden. Introductory manual explains laws of measurement in simple terms and offers tips for achieving accuracy and minimizing errors. Mathematics of measurement, use of instruments, experimenting with machines. 1994 edition. Foreword. Preface. Introduction. Epilogue. Selected Readings. Glossary. Index. Tables and figures. 128pp. 5⅜ x 8½. 40451-X

DALÍ ON MODERN ART: The Cuckolds of Antiquated Modern Art, Salvador Dalí. Influential painter skewers modern art and its practitioners. Outrageous evaluations of Picasso, Cézanne, Turner, more. 15 renderings of paintings discussed. 44 calligraphic decorations by Dalí. 96pp. 5⅜ x 8½. (Available in U.S. only.) 29220-7

ANTIQUE PLAYING CARDS: A Pictorial History, Henry René D'Allemagne. Over 900 elaborate, decorative images from rare playing cards (14th–20th centuries): Bacchus, death, dancing dogs, hunting scenes, royal coats of arms, players cheating, much more. 96pp. 9¼ x 12¼. 29265-7

MAKING FURNITURE MASTERPIECES: 30 Projects with Measured Drawings, Franklin H. Gottshall. Step-by-step instructions, illustrations for constructing handsome, useful pieces, among them a Sheraton desk, Chippendale chair, Spanish desk, Queen Anne table and a William and Mary dressing mirror. 224pp. 8⅛ x 11¼.
29338-6

THE FOSSIL BOOK: A Record of Prehistoric Life, Patricia V. Rich et al. Profusely illustrated definitive guide covers everything from single-celled organisms and dinosaurs to birds and mammals and the interplay between climate and man. Over 1,500 illustrations. 760pp. 7½ x 10⅛. 29371-8

Paperbound unless otherwise indicated. Available at your book dealer, online at **www.doverpublications.com**, or by writing to Dept. GI, Dover Publications, Inc., 31 East 2nd Street, Mineola, NY 11501. For current price information or for free catalogues (please indicate field of interest), write to Dover Publications or log on to **www.doverpublications.com** and see every Dover book in print. Dover publishes more than 500 books each year on science, elementary and advanced mathematics, biology, music, art, literary history, social sciences, and other areas.